JOHANNA

JOHANNA

JOHANNA

RITA L. MCWHORTER

LUMINARE PRESS
WWW.LUMINAREPRESS.COM

Johanna
Copyright ©2019 Rita L. McWhorter

Printed in the United States of America

Cover Design: Melissa K. Thomas
Illustrations by Diane McWhorter

Luminare Press
442 Charnelton St.
Eugene, OR 97401
www.luminarepress.com

LCCN: 2019917181
ISBN: 978-1-64388-178-2

*To the memory of our ancestors Johanna and Gregor
Hytrek and the other Nebraska Homesteaders.
They left comfortable homes in Europe to face unknown
hard times in order to settle on land that would
be passed to the next generations.
They earned our recognition, our respect,
and our gratitude.*

FOREWORD

In July 2003 we had a Hytrek Family reunion in our hometown, Stuart, Nebraska. When I returned home I wrote these words:

"When we see each other we remember how fervently we love each other and we renew that love. We remember our childhood and how much we respected and loved our parents. We acknowledge that we owe our beginnings to John and Theresa and other Hytreks, their wives and husbands, who gave up a comfortable life in a civilized world to scratch out a living on a lonesome prairie. It was their moral teaching, their determination and their hard work—and their ability to keep a sense of humor and to hold on to their music—that we value. No wonder our reunions are such great celebrations."

That reunion made me realize that many of the younger family members were not aware of how hard it was for the Homesteaders who came here in 1886 to begin to turn the prairie into what it is today. I wanted to write a book about them but I knew how hard it would be.

In 2004 my niece Bobbi King made a trip to Obrowiec, Poland, the small town our Grandparents Johanna and Gregor and other Hytreks came from. Her enthusiasm relit my interest and I decided to write their story. Bobbi supplied a skeleton of dates and names to work from. Later she sent copies of the actual Homestead papers they signed and updated. Bobbi, as the family genealogist, has always been a supporter who has encouraged me to continue writing until the book is finished.

Our family also owes a great debt to Marie Kramer and her daughter Judy. Marie is the author of "Homestead Fever," a book I call my bible because it is the most authoritative book on Homesteaders of this area. Both she and Judy helped me get started and were always available to help me out when I needed them. I also used information from another homestead descendant's story, "The Way I Heard It" by Raymond C. Dlugosh, as well as many other publications including "The Children's Blizzard" by David Laskin.

It took me a long time to get the story going but once I got really inside writing Johanna's story it was a delight. The various writing groups in my life during that time were more important than I can say. There is no way I can thank all of them for their help and support. My hope is that they enjoy reading the book and join me in the satisfaction we feel when we get our projects finished.

Changes in my life made it difficult as the end of the story came near and I became unsure that I could finish. Then my daughter Diane McWhorter knew just the kind of urging and gentle pushing I needed to get me back on track. She took over the job of arranging to get the book published, something I didn't have the energy to even think about. Without her recognizing that I needed her help the manuscript might have stayed in my file cabinet waiting to be discovered after I was gone. She deserves recognition for being the generous human being that she is. Thanks and Blessings on all our families of today, of the 1880s Hytrek homesteaders of Nebraska and our ancestors of long ago.

I wanted to hear Johanna tell her own story so she receives a blank book to write in as a gift just before they leave Poland for America in July of 1886. She writes almost daily as she travels from their home with her husband

     Rita L. McWhorter

Gregor and their three children. She relates the heartbreak of leaving family and friends, being seasick and fearful in the midst of crossing the Atlantic Ocean, and riding halfway across America in old passenger cars connected to a slow freight train. On August 10th they reach Stuart, Nebraska, the site of their homestead. They have come with a group of other Homesteaders who help each other build their sod houses. Gregor is reunited with his twin brother Stanislaus and their older brother Fritz (Frederick) who have been in America for about three years. Stanislaus is not married. Fritz has a wife, Marianna, and several children.

We follow them until they are faced with the worst experience of their lives, the Blizzard of 1888, a storm so wicked it is known for its fury and cold to this day. Although the book ends here, Johanna and Gregor accept their difficult challenges. They speak of their love for each other and their family and renew their determination to continue their life on the prairie.

CHAPTER 1

Johanna Hytrek
My Book

June 5, 1886:

We Are Going to America! The decisions are made, and the arrangements are in place. My husband Gregor and I, with our three children, will soon be sailing on a steamship to America to start a life of peace where Europe's wars cannot reach us. It seems so right to make my first entry in this new book as I am about to embark upon the greatest adventure I can imagine.

Since Poland is now ruled by Germany, when the Emperor went to war with France, Gregor, his twin brother Stanislaus and their older brother Frederick were forced to serve in the German army. Frederick, especially, found this duty hateful and his resentment grew so powerful that about ten years ago when he came home on leave he took off his uniform, threw it in a corner and exclaimed, "Well, that's enough of that! I am going to America!"

We were all worried, lest he be caught and punished, but he went without luggage and sneaked out of the country. We first heard from him after he made his way west to Missouri. Stanislaus left then to join his brother. About the time Gregor and I were married in 1880, the two brothers went to eastern Nebraska. By then Frederick was married to Marianna and they had two children. Three years ago they went to Holt County, Nebraska to homestead and we began to read their letters of encouragement and hope. Their sister Magdelena and her husband Frank Frost added their voices, and convinced us both that homesteading is the best thing to do, not just for us, but for the future of our children. So when we saw the sign announcing an Agent from America would be at a meeting about Homesteading, we went to listen. We signed the papers soon after and prepared to leave Obrowiec.

The best lure is the free land just waiting for us. In return we must commit to remain there and work the land for five years. You can also buy land, all you can afford. Here it is already owned and cut into smaller and smaller portions with each succeeding generation.

We have also learned that we are going to a land of free- dom. Our country once was Poland, but now it is Prussia. In America we will be in the State of Nebraska in the County of Holt near a new town named Stuart. There is no Emperor, or King or Queen who wants to have a war to change that freedom. Frederick, especially, speaks in every letter of the freedom he feels now that he no longer carries the constant worry that he will be called again to go to war. Gregor also is anxious to be free of that heavy fear.

Here in Obrowiec we have a nice church and no prob- lem with being Catholic, but in this unstable area that could change. In America you can practice whatever religion you wish. In Stuart there are many Catholic settlers from Poland, Germany, Austria and Slovakia, and probably other countries, too. We have been assured there is a church in a

    Rita L. McWhorter

neighboring town, and with so many new Catholics moving in, surely a fine new church will be built in Stuart. And a school! Soon there will be a school within walking distance where the children will learn to read and write in English.

Yes, I get carried away with my enthusiasm. Mama tries to warn me. "Think how hard it will be to start with nothing," she says. "You will have no house. Do you really think you can live in a dirt hole? And where will you go for flour and sugar? How far away? How will you get there?" She scolds because she is worried about us, and does not want us to move away. Gregor teases her, tells her that she is just jealous, and that she should come with us. Soon she is laughing at such foolishness, and forgets her worry. She has faith in Gregor and in me, and knows that we have made the right decision.

June 25, 1886:

At first when we told Mama and Papa Sapok that we are going to America and taking my son Roman with us, they cried and begged me to leave him with them. They had lost their only son, my first husband, and now to lose their only grandson was more than they could bear. After they accepted that Roman belongs with me and our family, Papa Sapok decided we should sell the tavern. My first husband and I had run the tavern, and when he died, I inherited his half-interest in it. Then I took over until Gregor came to help. It seemed a shame to give it up, but I agreed with Papa it would be best. Fortunately it sold quickly to one of our best customers. When we tried to give Mama and Papa their share of the money, they insisted we keep most of it to use to help pay for our passage, and all the things we will have to buy when we get there. It was for Roman, they said. They seem more at peace, now. I believe it is because they feel they have a stake in Roman's future.

July 4, 1886:
Again we unpacked everything and managed to squeeze in a few more things. It is difficult that we can take only the necessities. We have two wooden crates and two trunks all jammed full, but when we repacked there was still no way to find room for Gregor's accordion. We will sorely miss his music, but hope we will be able to buy a new instrument for him before long. Gregor says it sets a good example for the boys to know that we all must leave some of our favorite possessions in Poland.

July 11, 1886:
Today was our last Sunday in Obrowiec. This morning I directed the choir through my tears, and everyone did their best to stifle their sobs as we sang our last amen together. After Mass the whole town brought food for a reception for us, and we all struggled to stay cheerful as they spoke of their happiness for us. Father Pietrzyk made a big production of giving us the money from the collection. Then Gregor made a nice speech of thanks and said we could not accept it. So Father then gave the money to Roman, who didn't know what to do. Everyone clapped and said yes, yes, we should take it. Finally we did. It was such a touching, generous show of love and friendship.

On our way home we decided to visit the graveyard. Roman doesn't remember his Papa, of course, but we had always put flowers on the grave and told him about his father. Now he wanted to say goodbye. I wasn't prepared for how

　　　　Rita L. McWhorter

sad that visit made us feel. I had always taken for granted we would be buried here beside our family members.

Tonight we went to the tavern to say a final goodbye. This was not a time for serious talk or tears. The beer was freely flowing, and the toasts went on and on. Gregor seemed so carefree and happy as he played his accordion. Only I seemed aware that it would be for the last time. Of course I had to sing the old songs as I always have in the past. Everyone joined in and the party lasted late into the night.

But now at home, I am sorry I did not have a few quiet minutes alone with my best friend. I promise I will send a letter to thank her, my dear Stella, for this lovely book. It is with excitement and joy I write this, and also with sorrow. Gregor and I will have a new life with our family, but the cost is dear. Yes, the good wishes and presents from our family and wonderful friends send us off in good spirits. Our sadness lies in knowing we may never see any of them again in this life and that thought remains unrecognized and unspoken. If we were to speak of it, I would not be able to leave, for deep inside my heart is breaking. Only my belief in God and my faith in Gregor can bring me through. Goodbye Stella. I will never forget the friend whose name my daughter carries. Goodbye my country, goodbye my family, goodbye my friends. I love you. Pray for us. Pray for me.

CHAPTER 2

Off to Hamburg
and Beyond

July 14, 1886:
Although the parting from our friends and family was
so hard, once we got on the train we were relieved to be
embarking on our great adventure at last. Only Gregor had
ever been on a train before, so the boys and I were fasci-
nated with looking out the windows as everything went by.
So fast! We discovered that most of the others on the train
are going to America, too. As we talked to them our excitement built so that all we could think about was our future.

July 16, 1886:
I felt mature and strong when we left our home. After all
I am 32 years old and my eldest son is eight. I knew happiness when I married my first husband, delight when
Roman was born, and grief when his father died. Life
began again for me as a bride with Gregor, and soon I was
a mother again with the birth of our son Paul. And only a
little more than a year ago, our daughter Stella arrived. But
today everything was strange, frightening, and I wondered,
"Will I be able to do this?"

            Rita L. McWhorter

My confusion began here in Hamburg, Germany. We will soon sail from here to America. We thought our passage was all arranged, but were told that we must go to a certain place to check everything and sign papers before we can go. When we got there, it was so hot and crowded I thought I would faint. Roman was a blessing and tried to hold Paul by the hand, but Paul was so frightened he hid in my skirt and wouldn't let go of my leg. There was nothing Roman could do but try to act grown up and brave. Plump little Stella grew heavy in my arms. She squirmed and fought, but I dared not put her down. I stood by Gregor like a post, and the babble around me sounded like chickens in a crowded pen. Not a word could I understand. Not a word could I speak. I felt five years old and lost without my mama. While Gregor tended to our passports, little Paul was shoved by the crowd and fell to his knees. A stranger, good Samaritan to be sure, picked him up, tenderly brushed him off and gave him back to me with a smile. Thank you, I said in Polish. He ducked his head in a small bow, and answered in a language strange to me. His kindness was like a ray of sunshine.

July 18, 1886:
We are aboard our ship, the SS Suevia, which is making ready to sail. I am determined to enjoy our ocean trip. I told Gregor it was to be a vacation. He laughed at me and gave me a happy hug. We have a small cabin, crowded with the five of us, but I am grateful for our good accommodations. We are thankful to the agent who helped make the arrangements, for he told us we must have a cabin if we could possibly afford it.

Never could I have imagined the excitement of leaving the pier. A band was playing, people were waving, tossing flowers, laughing and crying at the same time. The ship is huge! How can it float? Gregor says to stop worrying. I will try.

July 20, 1886:
I have been so sick, but Gregor is worse. We had some bad weather and I am not feeling well enough to write.

July 21, 1886:
I am feeling much better, perhaps because I must. I dare not lose my milk, for who would nurse Stella? The ship went up, down and side to side all at the same time, but I was too sick to worry that we would sink. Thank God the children thought it was a game. They tumbled around laughing while Gregor and I covered our mouths and took turns going out to throw up. They even ate. It seemed like they were hungry all the time and we couldn't even think of food. But as mama always says, the bad times make you appreciate the good. Thank you for your wisdom, Mama. As soon as I can, I will send you a letter. It seems so long since we saw you.

It is a blessing that I have plenty of milk, for now I have two babies to care for. There is a couple in a cabin near us named Josef and Franceska Dlugosh. They are traveling with several children including a baby also named Josef. Poor Franceska is so seasick she has not been able to keep anything down for several days, so Joe brings little Joe over to me, and I nurse him along with Stella. I am glad I am able to help out, but I am worried about her.

July 22, 1886:
Thank goodness Gregor is better. Roman and Paul love to go out on deck and watch the waves. They come rushing back to tell me when they see a big fish. I go with them now

     Rita L. McWhorter

and then, but the waves are so big that I feel I am better off inside, keeping my stomach settled. The boys have made friends with the Dlugosh children, Johan, Anna and Frank. There is also a younger girl named Hedwig, and of course the baby. Franceska is not at all well, so I am still nursing the baby. He is such a sweet baby, and no trouble at all. Stella thinks he is her very own little brother. Gregor says they will be settling near us, so we already know one of our neighbors even though we are far out at sea.

August 1, 1886:
It is amazing that we have come such a long way in only two weeks. When I think of the people who made the trip by sailboat long ago, I can't imagine their hardship. We are spoiled by all the conveniences.

Tomorrow we will be on land again. I don't know if I am more excited or afraid. Gregor keeps reassuring me that all will be well, and that before we know it we will be in our new home where his brothers and family await us. So I say my rosary every night and pray that all will be as he says.

CHAPTER 3

Arrival in America

August 2, 1886:

I am exhausted. It is now quiet here but I cannot sleep. Although I am sure I will never forget our first day in America, I feel I must write it down.

The ship docked at Castle Garden, New York. We soon learned it was neither a castle nor a garden; it seemed to be a massive mess. Someone said it was an old fort built near the port where we docked.

Back when we signed the agreement to homestead, we were promised that Government Agents would be in America when we landed. They kept their promise. The agents moved through the crowd, miraculously sorting individuals by destination and uniting us with our belongings from the ship. The children and I stayed with our trunks and boxes while Gregor signed the papers to allow us into the country. He also changed some of our money into the money used in the United States.

The dock area was crowded with people, and the loud babble of many languages was like nothing we had ever heard before. We grew hot and thirsty, hungry and tired. What a relief it was when we were able to leave the so-called castle and go outside for a breath of air.

       Rita L. McWhorter

Our spirits revived as we rode into the city on a large carriage pulled by horses that the agent called a trolley. New York is a city like none we have ever seen and probably will never see again. There are churches, tall buildings, rows of buildings, hundreds, maybe thousands, of buildings of all sizes and descriptions crowded together, but none that look like ordinary houses. The streets are full of horses and carriages and people, people, people everywhere. We could not believe our eyes.

We were taken to Grand Central Depot where we will spend the night. This is the place that should be named a castle. It is like a spacious palace we might read about in a book but never expect to see. The floors are marble, and stately columns rise high to the ceiling far above. Some people were standing in lines to buy tickets, but all the rest were rushing, rushing. We sat with the children, silent and overwhelmed with awe.

When the crowd subsided, Gregor and the boys went into the men's washroom, and I took Stella with me to the one for women. Here was unbelievable luxury: shiny faucets with running water, and toilets that flushed the waste down the drain. Everything was clean and beautiful making it pure pleasure to wash Stella and myself.

When we came out to meet Gregor, Roman and Paul, my heart lifted to see them clean and bright with their wet hair carefully combed. I laughed and told them we should call this our Welcome to America celebration. Gregor smiled in agreement, gallantly offered his arm, and escorted us to the restaurant.

Our table had a white cloth and there were linen napkins tucked next to the plates. Glasses filled with water and gleaming silverware were carefully placed. After the waiter took the chits we had received from the agent for the meal, he brought a meat and vegetable stew with bread and butter. For dessert he served apple pie, coffee and milk. It all tasted delicious. Gregor left some of our new American coins for the waiter. How did he know he should do that? He must have watched what the others did.

After our exhausting day and elegant evening it was easy for Gregor and the children to settle down on the blankets we folded on the benches. I am the one who remains sleepless, overwhelmed with emotion, happiness and worry whirling together in my brain. But now that I have written about it, perhaps I can sleep. I will calm myself and say my rosary in thanks that we are safe in America.

August 3, 1886:
While people from the ship were still sleeping on the benches around us, I was awakened early by Stella wanting to nurse. We quietly made our way to the washroom where I found my friend Franceska nursing little Joe and a few other women with their babies. For some reason we barely talked with each other. It seemed an almost sacred place, like the small room at our church with the baptismal stand in its center. In that room we women go with our babies during Mass and we communicate mainly by silently sharing our common condition. Then I remembered that the day we docked was Sunday, and we could not go to Mass. A feeling of homesickness swept over me as I thought of my choir in St. Marii Magdaleny Church back in Obrowiec. When I reached into my pocket for my rosary, I noticed several other women, beads in their hands, silently praying. I felt very close to them.

By the time we joined our families, a bustling crowd of well-dressed people had arrived. I assumed they were on

      Rita L. McWhorter

their way to work. I had never seen men wearing such fine suits and hats. So stylish! Even their shoes were shiny. There were fewer women. All wore lovely dresses and their hats were breathtaking. They hurried past us without looking our way, but we could not take our eyes off them.

Now we will have breakfast and soon after we will board the train. This is a grand experience for us, but we are eager to be on our way.

CHAPTER 4

All Aboard!

It is still light in late afternoon so I will catch up on my story:

The agent was there after breakfast and Gregor stood talking with him until the man had to attend to his duties. Gregor is the kind of person who asks many questions. He says he wants to know where he will end up before he jumps. I admire him for that.

Our heavier baggage was picked up and as we were led across many tracks to our train, Gregor said the agent had told him cars we would ride in were attached to a freight train. Since it would stop often along the way, it would be a long trip. We would have to sit up all the way, so we should look for wicker seats, not wooden ones, and sit next to a window. He suggested I put Stella in the seat next to me, the two boys in the next two seats, and he would sit behind us. That way we would have more room than if I started out holding the baby. So that is what we did.

Around noon the train chugged slowly out of New York City, and we all had our eyes glued to the windows watching the city pass by. As it got warmer, people began to put down the windows, so of course Roman and Paul had to do the same. Soon the window was all the way down and they were

     Rita L. McWhorter

putting their arms outside to cool off. Next it was their heads they would try to stick out. I didn't worry too much while the train slowly chugged along, but when it sped up, smoky wind and cinders were coming into the train. I thought it was very unsafe, so I made them close the window. They sat pouting until a man came down the aisle selling food and they forgot all about it. We got a meal packed in a small box. We learned that when there is meat between two slices of bread, it is called a sandwich. And we learned the English word for apple.

August 4, 1886:
Well, we all survived our first night on the train. I thought the children would never settle down last night, but after dark they were finally quiet and slept pretty well. Sleeping sitting up is not so good for adults.

This morning some women came aboard with fresh baked bread, warm sausages and hot coffee. There was milk for the children, and more apples. We didn't have English words to tell them and they didn't understand Polish, but surely they could tell from the way we gobbled up the food and smiled at them how much we enjoyed it.

We are crossing the State of Pennsylvania and will be in Pittsburgh tomorrow morning. We are going through mountains covered with dense forests, and it must have been very difficult to build the railroad. Some places they have even made a tunnel right through a mountain.

August 5, 1886:
We got to Pittsburgh this morning, but we had to stay on the train. We were there for only a few hours, but it was very warm and the time passed slowly, especially for the children. Quite a few people got off the train there, so at

least there is now room to move around a little more. We crossed a couple of large rivers on grand bridges built far above the water, but now it is raining and there is nothing to see but thick forests that stretch out forever.

We are becoming well acquainted with the others in our car, especially the Dlugosh family. The men have figured out that their homestead must be very near ours, so they will be our neighbors. The boys especially like John, who is about their age. Anna is six, and has a bad foot so she cannot always join in with the rowdy boys. She likes to sit and visit with me. According to Anna, Frank is four years old, Hedwig is three and the baby Joe is only a few months, maybe six months, she thinks.

"Mamma is pregnant, you know, and that doesn't make things any easier for her. She doesn't know what she would do without you to help feed the baby. There is no milk to speak of on the train, and who knows if it is fresh?" Yes, she is quite the little mother.

Everyone is getting used to our life moving across the country–the puffing engines, the wailing whistle, the clackety-clack of the wheels going over the tracks. Even the little ones lurch down the aisles without falling, chattering with everyone who will pay attention to them. We women talk together and take turns entertaining the young ones with games, songs and stories, while the men move into groups of their own.

The government agent who travels with us is Hank Schueler. He and Gregor have become good friends. It was interesting to overhear them talking when Gregor asked him why the trip was taking so long.

"In the Old Country maybe you traveled across Poland," he said. "The country of Poland is like one state in the

             Rita L. McWhorter

United States. If you thought the United States was a country the size of Poland, you would not be prepared for such a long trip. Before we get to where you are going we must cross more than five states as big or bigger than Poland and then go half way across Nebraska."

When Gregor told him about our fast train ride from Obrowiec to Hamburg, Germany, he said, "You were probably on a speedy passenger train. Here you are on a freight train, an old one at that, which stops at almost every station, and loads and unloads all kinds of freight. That is why it is so slow."

Then they talked about Chicago. Gregor wanted to know how much further must we travel? Is it a large city? Would we stop there for long?

"From Pittsburgh we cross Ohio and Indiana before we reach Chicago," Hank said. "Chicago is not large like New York City, but it is growing fast. It has a good slaughterhouse business going there. After you are settled you may decide to sell cattle or hogs that will go to Chicago to be processed."

"But will we stop in Chicago for long?" I asked. The men didn't realize I had been listening, but Hank turned around with a smile.

"Not for long," he said. "But we have to change trains there, so you will have time to use the station to clean up a little and get a hot meal. It will be a nice change for you."

The men can talk about slaughtering cattle all they want, but Hank knew what interested me the most. We are able to buy food from people who come aboard the train from time to time, so we aren't going hungry. But staying clean is another matter. There is a very small room with a toilet at the end of the car, and a large can of water with a dipper to drink from just outside the door. It is possible to dip a little water into a basin, but if people use too much the can is soon empty and there is nothing to drink. It is especially hard to deal with Stella. The toilet opens straight to the ground between the rails, and even though I hold her, she is afraid to go. Later she makes a mess in her diaper. No, it is not easy, but we women help each other, so we will manage.

August ?:
I have lost track of the date. Everyone is tired and bored. How we wish for Gregor's accordion.

Yesterday I asked Gregor if Hank could organize a little run for the children now and then when the depot stop was long enough. Hank agreed. It is a life saver. The children romp, run and jump; then return flushed and breathless. Mothers, who have strolled about, are grateful for this short breathing space.

We are crossing the two states of Ohio and Indiana. Except for the small towns at the stations, we do not see much except a few farm buildings here and there. The fields of grass look lovely interrupted by those planted with corn and ripening grain, but we don't see many people.

August 8, 1886:
Stella is napping now so I can write. Yesterday we got to Chicago and were able to go into the station. It was not as grand as the station in New York City, but it was beautiful to see and we were grateful to spend a little time there. We headed straight for the washrooms where I thought we would never get enough of the precious running water. We drank and drank, enjoying its clean fresh taste. Stella laughed as I bathed her and put on fresh clothes. Quickly I rinsed her soiled ones for later. Then, although I felt shy

     Rita L. McWhorter

with so many people around, I unbuttoned my blouse and took it off. I soaped my breasts, my arms, and face and rinsed them well. When the other women from our train saw me acting so brave, they joined me and we giggled with the joy of it.

Again we were given a chit for a meal, and we enjoyed beef, potatoes and fresh garden vegetables with a nice pudding for dessert. Roman ate his pudding so fast that Gregor couldn't hide a smile. Then he pretended he was too full to eat his own and offered it to Roman. It was gone in a moment. Gregor put his arm across Roman's shoulders and they shared a good laugh. Paul didn't think it was a bit funny, so I ended up with no pudding myself. Before long we were all laughing together and everyone was looking at us.

Too soon we were back on the train, moving down the tracks again. I thought it would be different, but it was the same old car, only hooked onto a different train. Oh well, it did seem to have been swept, the toilet was cleaner and the water was fresh. As Paul says, the same old poketa, poketa, poketa over the rails.

August 9, 1886:
Our next stop is Omaha in the State of Nebraska, later today. From there we will proceed on the final part of our trip. We are all very tired. Last night after the children had settled down I started a song. Gregor added his fine strong voice, and soon many others in the car were singing along, softly, so as not to disturb the children. We have thought so many times on this hard trip, "If only Gregor had his accordion."

The singing made us a little homesick, I think, but Hank came to our rescue. He taught us a song about our new country. We had no trouble learning the melody, but the English words were hard for us. Hank explained "sweet land of liberty" and "let freedom ring." I will never forget that song. I sang it over and over in my mind as I drifted off to sleep.

This morning I sat with Stella asleep in my arms watching the scenery gradually change as we crossed Illinois. There were fewer trees, and more grass, "prairie," Hank said. He and Gregor were talking together again, in the seat behind me. Gregor thought the land itself looked somewhat like the countryside in Poland, but he couldn't figure out why all the towns seemed to be about the same distance apart.

"When the railroad was built through the prairie, ten miles was a day's work," he said. "So a small station was established at the end of every day with a water tank, a coal storage place or whatever was needed, and they set up camp for the night. At some stops a few of the people following the railroaders dropped off, and a town was born. Homesteaders are usually dropped off at a station that has a telegraph so we can communicate with them and arrange for each homesteader's needs. That's why you and those settling near you will get off in Atkinson. Stuart is about ten miles west of there, and the train goes on well beyond that. My responsibility is to see that each homesteader receives everything he has coming to him, and understands where he will meet our local representative."

"Will you...?" Hank interrupted before Gregor could think of how to ask his next question.

"Mr. Francis Frost is our representative in Stuart. I believe you are related to him in some way?"

"My sister Magdelana is married to Frank."

"Well, then, you have no worries. You will be well taken care of, I am sure."

     Rita L. McWhorter

I knew Gregor had more questions, but Hank moved on. There was lot of time to think on this long train ride, and we all had questions that had not occurred to us when we were back home.

Gregor came to sit beside me. He put his arm across my shoulders and we rode along in silence. As we got further into Iowa there was almost nothing but prairie. More and more families we had gotten to know got off and the stops became long and frequent. Sometimes we would see a family heading away with a team of horses pulling a new wagon full of boxes and supplies and I wondered, "To where?" "To what?" I did not want to face the answer. I knew the "where" was across the prairie which stretched out forever without a single house or even a small tree that might offer a little shade on a hot day. I didn't believe any of us really knew the answer to the question, "To what?"

As I watched, I could hear Mama's voice saying, "Think how hard it will be to start with nothing. You will have no house. Where will you get sugar, or coffee?" Those practical questions did not seem important then, but I suddenly became overwhelmed with worry. Will we really live in a dirt hole without the things we will need?

"Gregor," I asked "Where will we get our water?" Then dozens of question flooded my mind and tumbled out of my mouth. I could not stop.

My husband turned to me and took my hand. He looked into my eyes and smiled his kind smile. Stella stirred from her sleep. Gregor gently pushed the damp hair back from her hot forehead.

"You worry too much, Johanna," he said. "Frank will be there. Stanislaus is there. Fritz and Marianna live nearby. Everything will be all right."

After he moved away to talk to the other men, Franceska came over with little Joe. "Don't forget that I will be nearby, too." We chatted about how glad we were to have gotten so close to each other during this difficult time. She told me she had heard me ask all those questions. She had questions, too, "but we will have plenty to do just to worry about the children," she said. "Let the men worry for a change." Just as she said it, Joe began to cry. Stella took one look at him and cried even louder. I caught Franceska's eye and we began to laugh. Maybe the little ones know more than we do, I thought.

Rita L. McWhorter

CHAPTER 5

Stuart, Nebraska

August 10, 1886:

So much has happened that I can hardly believe it was only yesterday morning that I last wrote. Even more unbelievable is that we have survived the long, hard trip from Obrowiec, Poland to Stuart, Nebraska. If I had known how hard it would be, I would not have had the courage to leave home.

As we continued through Iowa we had to say goodbye to many people as they got off the train. They were all so happy and excited to be at their destination that we couldn't be sad to see them go. Roman sat with me complaining about all his new friends who were leaving the train. Paul squeezed in between us and put his head in my lap. Two tired, sad little boys.

"Let's talk about the family who is in Stuart waiting for us. Uncle Frederick."

"Fritz. Papa says they call him Fritz. Rosie. She's about my age," Roman is remembering.

"And John is about my age. Same as John Dlugosh?"

"I guess so, Paul. Who's next?"

"Twins! A boy named Joe and a girl. What's her name?"

"Frances."

"I thought that was a boy's name."

"Sometimes it is, but it's spelled different. Any more?"

"Another boy, William."

"Any more?"

"The mama. Mary something."

"Aunt Marianna. And maybe a brand new baby. Don't forget the other twin."

"Oh yes, Papa's twin brother. Uncle Stanislaus."

We stopped only briefly in Omaha where we changed trains for the final time. The train chugged its way west through the night and people continued to get off at what seemed like every stop. We slept fitfully. There were millions of stars, and a bright moon lit up the countryside, but between the stations there was nothing to see except the flat, empty prairie.

This morning, as Hank had promised, we got off the train at the Atkinson station. As we rubbed the sleep from our eyes, yawned and stretched our tired, cramped bodies, a group of local people brought breakfast. Some went aboard the train to sell their boxes for ten cents, which was the accepted contract, but those who served us were Polish women from the local Catholic Church. They chatted with us as they poured coffee, hot and strong, into cups and mugs. There was cream and sugar for the coffee, milk for the children, and delicious pastries and bread, warm and fresh. I wanted to know all about the church, about the town, about everything! But suddenly Hank was giving orders and we had to listen.

We were separated into groups according to our destination. There was quite a large number of people in the group that was going to Stuart. I realized then how fortunate we were; some of the families had long distances to travel, often by themselves.

     Rita L. McWhorter

When we arrived in Stuart, several of the others were already here, wondering where we should congregate for the night. We were just outside of town near the river, and one place looked as good as another to us. We all just stopped where we were. Soon we were getting out snacks for hungry children, serving a drink of water, or wiping a hot, dirty face with a cool cloth, and chatting together. The men and the bigger boys were going for wood for a fire, strolling into town to take their first look or unhitching the horses for those of us ready to stay where we were. Even though it was late afternoon, the sun was quite high in the sky, and it was still hot. In spite of that, everyone was in a good mood. We were relieved that the long trip was over, and we were excited about the next day. We would see the piece of land where we would make our homes. The land we had been promised would be ours.

I am now sitting next to our new wagon where there is a bit of shade. Stella is already settled on a blanket under the wagon, completely worn out. The boys are playing with Johan, Anna and Francek Dlugosh, and the other children. The energy pent up from the long rides on the boat and the trains is now unleashed. They cannot seem to get enough of all this freedom, running, shouting, laughing, pushing and jostling. The men, sensing the mothers need a break, are keeping their eyes on them, watching so the play doesn't get too rough. When they feel it is time, they send the children to us to clean them up, quiet them down and ready them for sleep.

The voices of the women are getting softer, and the men, now quiet and thoughtful, are smoking their pipes. There is comfort in the ending of a day. The huge ball of sun has flattened and then has set in an almost cloudless sky. The few white wisps brave enough to venture near the heat have turned to gold, then flamed to red before they gradually cooled. They still persist, long after the sun is gone, pink and paling to violet and blue. I was not prepared for the beauty of the Nebraska sunset. It should be in the song Hank taught us along with the spacious skies.

Speaking of song, on the way here today I heard the most beautiful bird. He was of medium size, brownish on the back, with a bright yellow throat and breast, elegantly set off with a black collar just below the neck. He was perched on a sturdy stem which rose above the prairie grass, swaying a bit in the wind, a beautiful sight. What really caught my attention was his song. It was a rich warble of clear notes down the scale and then a loud, flute-like trill that no human voice could duplicate. I know. I tried to sing it. I am eager to find out his name, for he is my favorite bird, even though I have not had a good look at any others. After less than one day in Nebraska, he has captured my heart. I believe he is a good omen.

August 11:
The roosters from the town woke us early, those of us who were not already stirring. The men and older boys had brought dry wood from the riverbank, and we had a fire to heat water for washing and for making coffee.

I asked Gregor why Frederick and Stanislaus were not here to greet us. He explained they wouldn't have known exactly what day we would get here, and reminded me to call his brother Fritz, here in the new land. He thought we would probably see them soon. We know that Frank Frost will soon be here to take charge of showing each of us where our land is.

It took us all a long time to go to sleep last night. Too much excitement. Gregor and I were stretched out on blan-

     Rita L. McWhorter

kets, the first time we have lain side by side for such a long time. Our bed was quite hard and lumpy, but after a cool breeze sprang up we slept well enough.

We didn't go into the town yesterday, but from the talk around the campfire this morning I gather everyone is very friendly. According to Joe, who went to town with Johan, two or three years ago Stuart had around 400 people. Back then stores and businesses were building everywhere along the main street, and they even had an opera house. Then in January of 1884 a fearsome fire struck, and much of Main Street was destroyed. They are trying to rebuild, but many people lost all they had and moved away. One good general store is there now, another starting up and a lumber yard growing fast. There are two churches, Methodist and Presbyterian, but we will have to go to Atkinson to attend Mass. The people seem to be hardworking folks who are determined to build the town up beyond what it was, so surely there will be a Catholic Church, someday.

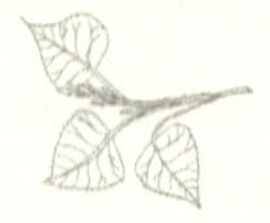

CHAPTER 6

Our Family

August 12, 1886:
As a new day dawns I write yesterday's story of our first day on the Nebraska prairie and my meeting with Fritz's wife, my sister-in-law, Marianna. It begins with all of us securing everything in our wagons. As soon as Frank got to our camp he led the way to our various homesteads. When we got to the first homestead, he said the women and children should stay with the wagon, while the men went with him until they got to the Dlugosh place, because the sod plow was on Joe's wagon. There they would learn how to use it to dig the sod for their house. Everything was so confusing to me that I couldn't realize just what he meant, but I soon found out.

When we got to our place, Gregor jumped out of our wagon and into the one Frank drove. "I'll be back soon," he said, and off they went. He looked back with a happy, excited grin, waved to us and left! And all the other wagons left as well.

We got down from the wagon and I stood there holding Stella, Roman on one side, Paul on the other. Alone.

I was panic-stricken. I wanted to get away but there was nowhere to go. There was nothing there, nothing but grass that stretched as far as I could see. It was deadly quiet and as empty as an ocean. Even the sky was empty except for

 Rita L. McWhorter

the sun that beat down unmercifully. I could not put Stella down in grass almost as tall as Paul. She could wander off in a minute and how could we find her? It was wickedly hot and there was no shade except under the wagon with the horses still harnessed to it.

"Dear God," I thought. "What have we done? I am a tavern keeper, not a farmer. What am I doing out here all alone?" The horses were feeding on the grass, slowly moving away, pulling the wagon with them. I needed to tie them to something, but there was nothing except the monotonous, silent grass that stretched to a far horizon, without a whisper of a breeze. There was not one tree. Not one post or pole or fence or house or road. Tears began to fill my eyes, tears of anger at Gregor for leaving me alone, tears of frustration, of doubt, of worry. Then I sneezed. On top of everything, the grass made me sneeze.

"I'm thirsty," Paul said.

"Will Papa come back?" Roman worried.

Stella struggled against my arms. "Down! Down!" she insisted.

The children's voices brought me back to reality. This was no time for such foolishness. As I fumbled for my handkerchief Fritz and Marianna drove up through the long grass in a jaunty buggy pulled by two lively horses.

Fritz barely embraced me, briefly patted the two boys on their heads, ignored Stella, and shouted, "Where's Gregor?"

I explained he had gone with Frank to learn how to use the sod plow.

"Hell," he cried. "I know how to use a sod plow. I own one. I'll fetch him back."

Marianna quickly gathered her skirts and jumped out of the buggy. Fritz handed down the baby bundled up in a blanket, grabbed the reins, and tore away across the field.

Marianna stretched out her hand to Roman and Paul. "I'm your Aunt Marianna," she said. Usually shy, the boys surprised me. Roman introduced himself and Paul, and cheerfully took her hand.

"And this is Stella," he said, taking his sister from me. "I'm seven, and I used to hold Stella when she was a baby. How old is your baby? What's his name?"

"His name is William. If you will all sit down here where we have tramped down the grass I will let you hold him for a little while. Be careful, though. He is only six weeks old."

Marianna took me into her arms in a soft embrace. Then I felt her arms tighten as though to share her own inner strength. "Johanna," she said, "dry your eyes. You have to be the brave one. It is not as bad as it looks."

I understood her words both spoken and implied. An angel straight from heaven could not have been so welcome a presence. I was speechless with relief and gratitude.

"Now come," she continued. "We will go to my house where you can rest. You'll soon feel more at home."

She loaded the baby, the children and me into our wagon, took the reins and drove the team through the grass. When I saw their place, I wondered why I hadn't seen it before. I suppose in my panic I couldn't think straight enough to turn around to look at what was only a short distance behind me. A healthy stand of many small trees stood near the sod house, and there were several other buildings to the south and west. As we got closer I could see a fenced enclosure where two cows lay comfortably chewing their cuds in the shade of a shelter that was attached to the barn.

We were greeted by her waiting children. They stood smiling but shy until their mother said, "Now what kind of a welcome is that for your Aunt Johanna and your cousins?"

     Rita L. McWhorter

Four sun-bronzed, barefoot children stood in a row on the sandy ground trying to be patient. Roman and Paul couldn't contain their excitement and jumped to the ground. The conversation leaped ahead of the introductions. "You must be Roman." "Are you Rosie?" "This is John." "I'm Paul." The twins would not be left out. The four-year-olds jumped and pushed shouting, "I'm Frances." "I'm Joseph." They repeated their names over and over until Roman and Paul gave them the attention they demanded.

Stella was out of my arms before I knew it, in the middle of it all. Rosie bent down and opened her arms. "Stella, Stella," she called. After a sisterly hug Rosie introduced her little brother William. In spite of Rosie's coaxing, the two shy little ones backed away from each other. When I got down from the wagon, Stella sought refuge behind my skirt while the others clustered around to welcome me. Such healthy, strong, happy children, I thought.

With barely a word from Marianna, Rosie took charge of the younger ones while John and my boys led the horses toward a hitching post where they tied them securely. I looked away from the children to the homestead. I was amazed at what Fritz and Marianna had accomplished in only three years. They had made a wonderful home here with crops growing all around, horses and cows, pigs and chickens, a corn crib, a shed, a barn and the sod house. But best of all, I thought, trees were growing to the west and north, and Fritz and the boys had already started building their new wooden house.

Mama's words came to me again as Marianna and I approached the soddie. "Do you think you can live in a dirt hole?" she had asked. I was about to see if such a thing was possible.

Of course it was not a dirt hole at all, but a fair-sized rectangular, sturdy looking house, although I had to admit the grass growing out of the roof did look a bit unusual. A strong, solid door was set into a wooden frame in the long east wall. I was surprised to see that the wall itself was very thick. Marianna gently pushed the door open and we entered a quiet, cool room that was lit by an open screened window on the south. I had expected it to be musty and dark, but the walls were white and the air was sweet. There was a rug on the floor made from feed and grain sacks, and the ceiling was hung with pieced cloths.

Marianna moved quickly to close the south window. "I like the fresh morning air," she explained, "but if I leave the window open too long it will become like an oven in here."

I followed her beyond a partition to the bedroom where there was another window to close. Mattresses were neatly stacked on top of the bed; clothing and bedclothes were stored on wooden shelves next to the walls. Every inch of space was carefully used.

Back in the main room I noticed that the window was set flush with the outside wall, making a wide window seat inside the room. The seat was covered with a bright cloth that matched the curtain that framed the window. It was one more bright touch that made it a cheerful, homey room. The partition between the two rooms was topped with a piece of smooth wood where several books were kept along with a beautiful lamp.

A few minutes later the two of us were sitting by the table sipping a cool, pleasant tea. Marianna nursed the baby until he went to sleep. After she put him down she mentioned her concern about Frank. "He is so much smaller than my other babies were, and he doesn't seem as strong as he should be."

 Rita L. McWhorter

This opened the conversation to having babies, as is usual when women get together, but I began to realize that out here things were much harder. There was no doctor, for one thing, and Marianna was the one who helped most of the women in the area.

"So who helped you with William and Frank?" The answer was that Fritz was pretty good at following her directions by now, and she usually had a fairly easy time of it. Even Stanislaus was a help. He took the children to his place the day the baby came, for both of the boys who had been born here. Rosie and John are very good with the younger ones. With all the new people moving in it will be easier. "We can all help each other."

I told her about Franceska being pregnant, and she said she would stop by to see her one day soon. She poured more tea.

"I've never tasted anything quite like the tea. What is it made of?"

"It is made from rose hips," she said. She smiled at my blank stare. "You will discover the prairie has many secrets. One is the wild flowers. There is a wild rose that grows here in sheltered, sandy places. It blossoms with the softest pale pink flower. Rosie has taught the boys where they thrive, so every June they bring me a bouquet. Then I have to kiss their sweet little fingers that are pierced with the thorns of the rose." She stops for a chuckle and a sip of her tea.

"I save the petals for the scent bags I make for my clothes trunk and to give for little presents. After the blossom drops off the bush, a seed ball grows in its place. That is the rose hip. I harvest them in late summer, to use in the rose hip tea you have just enjoyed." She reached for a nearby jar, and removed the lid. "Notice how sweet they smell."

Sudden tears stung my eyes and began to run down my cheeks. Crying and laughing at the same time I sobbed out the tale of Mama and her warning of living in a dirt hole, and here we were, two women who had never met each other, not even exchanged a letter, having tea together in this lovely room.

"Oh, Marianna," I sobbed. "How can I tell you..."

She patted my shoulder. "Go ahead and cry, Johanna. You have had such a long, hard journey. You will feel better after you have a good cry." She reached into a nearby bag for a small piece of clean cloth, and took one for herself. She held me loosely as we leaned toward each other in our chairs, and talked to me in low, loving tones, sometimes with tears, then with encouragement and finally with strength in her voice.

In a little while we dried our eyes, and Marianna took both my hands in hers. "Now we are truly sisters, glued together with rose hip tea. And a few tears."

Now you see why I was so eager to write about how I met Marianna. I would feel silly and weak this morning for having had a crying spell, if it weren't for her understanding. What a wonderful sister she is. Her kindness extended on through the day, to getting the things we needed from our wagon, to seeing to the meals, and finally to the evening when Stella and I both fell asleep over our supper. Marianna put down a mattress in the corner by the window in the big room where my baby and I slept until the first light of this sparkling new day. I was surprised to find Gregor sleeping beside me when we woke, for I had slept so soundly I hadn't realized he was there.

Stella and I crept quietly outside so as not to wake the rest of the family. We sat in a makeshift chair while Stella nursed, and listened to the farm begin to come to life. Here with Marianna's family, surrounded by build-

     Rita L. McWhorter

ings, trees and living creatures I am trying to understand my feelings about the prairie yesterday. What caused my panic when I stood there feeling all alone? Fear of isolation? Fear of loneliness?

I thought of my life in Obrowiec, always in the midst of family and friends, never alone. I knew everyone in the town, in the church and my heart ached to be back with them in the place I had known so well. No wonder I felt so lonely and afraid. But now that I see all that Fritz and Marianna have done in such a short time, I know that Gregor and I will soon have a place like this. And I know that not all our family is back in Poland, Fritz and Marianna have seen to that. Yes, our old friends are far away, but new friends are all around us, all of us facing the same challenges and helping one another.

Gregor and Fritz just drove away. They are going to O'Neill where Gregor will sign the first papers for our homestead. It is a long way to O'Neill, about 40 miles. On the way back they will pick up lumber for the door and window frames of our sod house, so it will be a long day for them.

"Today you will sign your life away at the County Courthouse," Fritz had teased. "You will have to declare it is your intention to become a citizen of the United States, and you will have to renounce your allegiance to the Emperor of Germany." Gregor is quick to say he won't have any trouble doing that. They were in good spirits, two brothers enjoying being together again.

I must put my book down now to see what I can do to help Marianna and pay attention to all she will teach me.

CHAPTER 7

From the Earth

August 13:

Yesterday, I was Marianna's shadow as she went about her work. We visited the barn, the chicken coop and the garden. It takes a couple of years to get a good garden, but there had been enough rain this year to raise nearly everything she had planted.

In order to cook the chicken she killed and dressed in the afternoon, Marianna started a fire in the small stove that sits outside the house to keep the house cool in the summer. The first thing I learned was that it is not easy to have a fire when you have no trees for wood, and I began to realize what it will be like for us to keep warm in the winter. Marianna used twisted hay and dried chips in her stove. Since I was a town girl and we had plenty of wood in Obrowiec, I was shocked to learn the dried chips were actually cow manure. Unbelievable to me, some of the chips were from the herds of buffalo that had lived here on the prairie not too long ago. Just the thought of handling animal manure to cook with made me want to go wash my hands. She also told me that the bleached bones that lie in the sandy places where the grass cannot grow are from the buffalo that roamed in large herds. They were killed for their coats and left to rot without regard for the Indians who had depended upon them for food. I cannot imagine such a thing.

While the chicken cooked in a large pot, we sat inside as we prepared the vegetables: carrots, small sweet onions, green beans, even a few early new potatoes, and we sliced large red tomatoes for the table. I had a garden at home, but learning to grow things in this sandy soil, to say nothing of knowing which plants are weeds, and which bugs are the harmful ones, will be another challenge.

The men arrived home before sunset and saw to the milking and feeding the animals. The children were still doing their chores, Rosie gathering eggs and feeding chickens with Frances, William and Stella. The boys were chasing pigs and trying to ride the calves, if you can call that doing chores. The men were tired and ready to wash up and rest. Washing up was no problem. They have a well near the house with a hand pump to bring the water up, and during the warm weather they use a crude wooden washstand. A pail of water stands there, a dipper hanging on its rim, and next to it is a basin and soap. Nearby is a post where a small cracked mirror hangs with a towel on another nail just below it. There is even a comb dangling from a piece of string.

Feeling refreshed, Fritz found his energy again. "This calls for a celebration," he said, inviting Gregor and me into the house. Marianna was already there getting out four small glasses. Fritz brought a brown bottle to the table and we all sat down. With a flourish he slowly poured the amber liquid into the glasses and we raised them on high. "Na zdrowie!" we said as we clinked them together.

"Once more," Fritz commanded as he refilled the glasses. This time Marianna raised her glass first. "To our new family, all eleven of us, and to our future together."

"How many times we drank a toast in the old days. Who could have guessed we would drink to our future in America," Gregor said as he raised his glass. "To our brother and sister who helped us decide to come here. Thank you." Then turning to me he said, "And to Johanna, a brave woman in a strange land." I wondered if he had learned how alone I had felt the day before.

Fritz changed the subject and told us they had stopped to see Stanislaus, whose place is not far from here. Gregor said his brother did not look at all well.

"He seemed so happy to see me that he was shaking and crying and didn't want to let go of me. I think he is too much alone, with only his dog for company. The war was very hard on Stanislaus. He told me he still hears the explosions and the guns."

Suddenly Rosie stuck her head in the door. "The stew is boiling, Mama. Time to drop the dumplings in." I guess in America, that means "Dinner is served."

After a good bit of jostling, pushing, spilled water, noise and laughter, seven shining, smiling faces emerged, eager for supper. The dumplings cooked quickly and the aroma from the chicken stew drew everyone close to the pot where our bowls were filled. We took our food inside and sat around the table where there was bread and butter, sliced tomatoes and fresh milk. The children scrunched down around a table of their own, an overturned wooden box. It is wonderful how they get along so well together. I think it is because of Rosie, at only eight years old such a good little mother to them all.

The boys were allowed to sleep in the loft of the barn. The mosquitoes are sometimes bad, but Fritz has built a wooden framework with a net for protection, and the hay

     Rita L. McWhorter

is comfortable to sleep on. They thought it an exciting adventure to sleep off by themselves.

Again our mattress was near Stella's in the corner of the big room close to the open window. After the house became quiet, Gregor told me he and Fritz had talked about my feeling so alone, as I had suspected, and he apologized for having been so thoughtless. It was wonderful to lie in a bed with my husband after what seemed a very long time.

We are up before dawn this morning. Today we will begin to build our house. Marianna has offered to keep Stella. When the men finish their chores, Roman, Paul and I will go with them to help our new home rise from the prairie.

CHAPTER 8

We Will Have A House

August 14:

When we got to our home site yesterday morning, Frank was already there. We knew generally where we wanted to put the house, but we walked around with Frank to find a place where the soil was the least sandy, the grass grew the thickest and the ground was level.

As the sun rose the neighbors began to gather, ready to work. With their scythes they began to cut the grass in the area Frank calculated was large enough for the house, and the sod needed to build it. A team of horses was hitched to that mysterious plow we had last seen in Joe Dlugosh's wagon. They plodded back and forth as the plow peeled off a three-inch slice of grass 15 inches wide and tipped it on its side, row after row. The man behind the plow worked hard to guide it and hold it steady. The sod was removed from the house site, and Gregor beckoned us over to the naked ground.

"Come here, boys, you can help mark where the walls of our house will be." First he helped Roman hold a huge hammer to pound in a wooden stake. Then it was Paul's turn to stake the next corner. Just then Roman saw that his Uncle Stanislaus had arrived.

"Uncle, Uncle, come help me pound in this stake," he called. Stanislaus was pleased and proud to be included.

When the stake was planted he shouted: "Fritz, I think Paul needs a little help over there." Uncle Fritz and Paul drove in the fourth stake. I had the honor of marking the front door. Two stakes! The hammer was heavier than I thought, but I drove both of them in by myself.

We used a ball of heavy twine to string a line between the stakes and the real work began. Gregor and I had to smile at the way the two boys swaggered away with their uncles to join the rest of the men.

The work crew was mainly the younger men among our neighbors. They had been working together for a couple of days now, and seemed to know just what to do. They cut the sod into 30-inch long "bricks" with their spades, a heavy load to handle hour after hour. They started by laying these sod bricks end to end on the bare ground, inside the line we had set up between the stakes for the 25 by 12 foot house. Another row was laid on the ground next to it, toward the inside, staggered so the seams did not meet, establishing a wall 30 inches wide. After a second layer was added, the third layer was laid across the lower two, "...tying them together," Frank explained. Roman and Paul steadied the door frame that was set in, and the men continued to stack the sod layers next to it.

The "old timers" who had settled here two or three years earlier had learned the best way to build a sod house in this area, so all of the houses for the group of us who had arrived together were built according to the same plan. The door and one window were on the long east wall, and one window on the south. That is because the cold winds come from the north and west, and most of the light comes in from the east and south. They found that building in a partition to offer even a small amount of privacy had proved to be worth the trouble.

When the walls were three or four feet high, the window frames were set in. A small space was left above the top of the door and windows to be filled later with grass or sacking. This would allow the sod to settle without damaging the frames.

When I turned around to see if Roman and Paul were keeping out of trouble, I saw them struggling together to carry a piece of sod to the wall, dirty sweat running down their flushed faces. Their father, uncles and the other men praised them for their muscles and their willingness to work. Before long they had found smaller pieces to carry, and the walls continued to rise.

All day the crew toiled in the blazing sun, taking turns to rest in the shade of the wagons for a few minutes. The wispy breeze that had been refreshing in the early morning had died away and there was little respite from the burning heat. I had never been a sky watcher, but now my attention was caught by the big, puffy white clouds floating in the startling blue sky. I imagined I could feel a moment of coolness as a cloud passed overhead. Also, patches of the prairie grass in the distance mysteriously changed color from time to time. I realized I was seeing the shadows of the clouds that moved over the prairie, and over us. Never before had I been aware of this simple fact of nature, that on a sunny day a cloud casts a shadow. As Marianna had told me, the prairie has many secrets to discover.

We had brought water, bread and vegetables from Marianna's garden that I served throughout the morning. In the early afternoon everyone stopped for a longer break.

     Rita L. McWhorter

Franceska came with coffee, bread and sausages, and more water for a quick wash-up to cool off as much as to get a little clean. The work didn't stop for long. Looking at the western sky we could see the puffy clouds I had admired had begun to accumulate, and there was talk that it might rain.

As the afternoon grew late Fritz said I should take the boys home. Getting caught in a lightning storm out in the prairie was dangerous. Gregor saw that Roman and Paul were slow to climb into the wagon with me. It was hard for them to become children again after having been treated as equals with the men. Gregor understood.

"See there, Uncle Stanislaus is already heading for home. All the men will be leaving very soon."

Paul climbed up on the seat beside me, and Roman sat on the floor with his legs dangling over the back of the wagon. Suddenly we hear his excited voice. "Stop, Mama. Stop and look back!" The sky had become dark and a strong breeze had sprung up. All around us the endless grass flowed in waves.

"It's like the ocean, the huge empty ocean, except for our house." He was right. Our house sat there by itself, sturdy and tall. Roman smiled and sat up straight. "We helped," he said.

"Yes, we helped," echoed Paul. "We helped a lot."

The clouds were becoming angry now. We could hear the rumbling in the west and we hurried to the farm. As the first drops began to fall Roman took over.

"Quick, Mama, go inside. We'll take the horses to the barn."

I gathered up what I could carry and hurried toward the house. As I watched to make sure they were safe, the first lightning struck with a crack of thunder in the west. It was so loud I felt a shock of fright, and the rain came teeming down. Thank God the boys had made it just in time, and

Fritz and Gregor came rushing by a moment later. They could all safely wait out the storm in the barn.

The door opened, and there was Marianna ready to help me in. The wind tore through the yard blowing the rain in a sheet before it. We slammed the door shut. Inside it was quiet and serene. Rosie was entertaining the younger ones with a game, and Stella came running to me. As I picked her up Marianna and Rosie began rushing around, putting bowls and pots here and there to catch the rain that began to leak through the roof. Even the twins tried to help, but it was of little use. The neat, pretty little place I had seen on my first day here was transformed. It was a mess. I stole a glance at Marianna to see how she was taking it.

"It's just a summer storm," Marianna said cheerfully as she could. "It will be over all too soon. And we need the rain."

In less than an hour it was over. When Rosie saw the sun was out she opened the door and ran outside. "Look for the rainbow, everyone, look for the rainbow!" Her bare feet danced in the wet sand and she raised her arms to the sky.

"The rainbow! The rainbow!" she sang. Our spirits lifted with hers to the beautiful colors that arched high and brilliant for a few moments before fading away.

The air was fresh and cool. Everything was soaked and washed sparkling clean. Even the boys were wet. They had been allowed to run out in the rain after the fury of the storm was spent.

Stanislaus came driving up. Noticing he was wet I asked, "Did you get caught in the rain?"

"No, not caught. I like the rain, and if I stay outside I know the noise is thunder. If I am inside it sounds like guns. I got home in time to pick the tomatoes. Marianna, these are for you." He put a huge basket of tomatoes on the wash bench.

     Rita L. McWhorter

Marianna was glad to have them with so many of us to feed.

When the chores were done we all gathered for the meal. Marianna asked Stanislaus to stay for supper. Everyone talked pleasantly together, but conversation seemed foreign to Stanislaus. He ate quickly, said thank you and left. Poor Stanislaus. We all worry about him.

August 14, 1886, Saturday:
This morning is glistening, pleasantly cool and the breeze that wafts over the prairie brings fragrant odors. Some days wind makes me sneeze and feel congested, but today is perfect. Stella is happy making hills and mountains in the sand near me.

It is too wet to finish the sod work on the house today, and tomorrow is Sunday. We will all go to church, and by Monday things will be well dried out. There is plenty to do. The door and windows must be installed. The floor must be walked down to make it smooth, and a coat of clay from the river spread on it. We will need lumber and tar paper for the roof before a layer of sod goes on top. And there are more houses to build. Gregor and his brothers will continue to work with the crew as much as they can until all the houses are mostly finished. I am hoping our house will be ready for us to move into soon. I feel we have imposed on Marianna too long already.

CHAPTER 9

Community

August 15, 1886, Sunday:
Today we got up very early to go to Church for the first time in America. "Oh, this is not a real church at all," I thought when we first entered the plain wooden building.

"Did you think it would be St. Mary Magdelana in Obrowiec?" I scolded myself. But truly, it didn't feel like a church.

I dipped my fingers in the holy water font and crossed myself. We approached an empty bench, genuflected, entered and knelt on a board to pray. An organ began to play and I quickly looked to see that a woman sat at the organ, pumping with her feet as her fingers found familiar chords, chords I know as well as I know my name. With that, in my mind everything changed. The rough benches became the smooth, varnished pews that I had left at home. The priest, familiar in an ornate robe, took his place at the altar. His servers, two young altar boys, knelt on either side. The Mass began, each Latin word clear to me.

"Kyrie Eleison," sang the priest. There was no choir to answer, so the organist responded in a lovely clear voice. I thought my heart would stop. How painfully I missed my church and my home. Gregor clasped my hand in his for a silent moment and handed me his handkerchief for my tears.

     Rita L. McWhorter

When the priest faced the congregation to give his sermon, he spoke in English, then in Polish to welcome all newcomers, and invited us to stay after Mass to meet new friends. I am ashamed to say I don't remember what he preached. I guess my eyes opened so wide my ears became deaf. There were simple pictures of the Stations of the Cross on the walls, beautiful linen on the altar, and hand-made candles. I noticed the people. The family next to us could have been the Cozakis who lived across the street from us in Obrowiec. One woman smiled kindly when she caught my eye. She bore a resemblance to Mama, I thought. I felt so homesick it took all my strength to keep back the tears. Roman looked miserable; Paul clutched my hand; Gregor held his handkerchief ready for use.

The Communion hymn brought my attention back to the Mass. The music was so familiar I nearly sang it aloud with the organist. But my practical self took over. No longer was I the choir director at St. Magdelana. I was mother and wife in America. I took a deep breath, and gathered my family. We left the church together.

As soon as we got outside the woman who had smiled at me spoke to us in Polish. Up close she didn't look anything like my mother, but she was very nice.

"I am so happy to see you here. I am one of the women who met your train a few days ago. You are from Poland, yes? Most of us here are from Poland, too. You must meet everyone. Yes, you children, too. You will find new friends here, and something good to eat." She led us to a room where tables were set up, with coffee and kolaches, every-one talking, children darting in and out through the crowd.

Before we knew it, it was well after noon and time to start for home. I bought a few things at the store while the men watered the horses, and we lunched on bologna and crackers as we bumped along the trail.

"The church is all right," Roman said, "but not like home. Maybe some day we will help build a big church with lots of pointy steeples and colored windows like we saw in New York City. But the people are nice. Some of the boys look almost like the boys in my school."

"And act like them, too," agreed Paul. "That one big kid Leo was pushing everybody around, just like Joe used to do." Roman asked if Paul was scared of him.

"Naw, when he came up to me and my new friend Frank, we left and went back for another cookie. He's BIG."

It was hot, and silence spread over us as we settled into the steady, plodding rhythm of the horses' hooves over the uneven ground. Suddenly I saw him: My bird! He flew across the field and perched on a tall stalk. He was as bright and beautiful as I remembered. I listened for his song, but he didn't sing. He just flew away. Gregor said he had noticed in Poland that birds didn't sing in late summer.

"There was a German fellow in the Army with me, Hans. He spoke a little Polish, and I learned a little German from him," Gregor said. The boys drew closer. They loved to hear Gregor's stories. "One day, I think it was in September, we saw huge flocks, thousands of birds together, fly overhead. I raised my gun like a hunter and said, 'Bam, bam.' Hans nodded in understanding and we laughed a little. I asked him where the birds were going. He told me that birds who eat insects have to fly south to get enough to eat when our weather turns cold. That sounded sensible to me, but I tried to stump him with another question: I hear the birds sing all the time, but not lately. Why don't they sing now?

            Rita L. McWhorter

'They don't have anything to sing about,' he answered. I thought he was joking, but he wasn't. 'In spring the male sings to attract a mate, then to protect his territory. Now he doesn't sing. He just gets fat and ready to fly.'"

"Papa, is that a true story?" You could never tell for sure about Gregor's stories. But this one was true.

"Your Meadowlark will sing for you next spring, Johanna. Oh, I guess I forgot to tell you I asked Fritz, and that is what he told me. Your bird is a Meadowlark."

It was a long trip home so we sang some of the old songs together to help pass the time. We had already migrated and didn't have to wait for spring to do our singing.

When Obrowiec was my world, I would sometimes hear the expression, "It's a small world." After crossing the ocean and half of America I am discovering how big the world really is. Finding a community so much like home so far away gives new meaning to the expression. How lucky we are to have these people so like us close by. Even now, writing in my book, I can smell the aroma of coffee and cinnamon, and feel the warmth of friendliness.

August 29, Sunday afternoon:
It has been two busy weeks since I last wrote. We are living in our house now, but are far from settled. We decided to use new lumber for the roof and the floors. The roof is on, the windows and door are installed, and the floors look wonderful. Putting the whitewash on the walls was a hard job, but it looks pretty good.

The men have put in a fence for our two new cows and the horses, and water from a well can be pumped into a large feed tank. Loading that big tank into the wagon and keeping it there for the ten mile trip out to here was quite a chore. We got to laughing about how it tried to get away from us. Was it trying to roll back to its home? It's a wonder we made it over the bumpy roads. We still laugh whenever we talk about it.

The well is fairly close to the house, so we pump our drinking water from it, too. Some day maybe we will have a deeper well and the water will flow out by itself to fill the tank. Roman is strong enough to carry a pretty good pailful from the well to the house, so that is a big help. Gregor has built a washstand in the house, and we have a new basin and soap dish. A slop bucket sits under the stand for the dirty water. I will need help emptying that, too. Plenty of chores for all!

Inside the house we have what is called a Buffalo Chip stove. It has a flat top and burns hay, wood or chips. A stove pipe takes the smoke out through a hole made in the roof, but while the weather is hot I cook outside over a little open fireplace Gregor and the boys made for me. We found a very nice table with two leaves and six matching chairs that I wanted so much, but there is no way it would fit in our little house. Even the small table and two chairs we bought take up a good bit of room. Two small stools fit under the table.

I quickly put together mattresses for us all, not very thick because there is nothing much to stuff them with, but they will do for now. Some day we will have feathers to stuff them with. Mattresses on the floor are enough for the children, but we will have to get a bed for Gregor and me. We need a better night's sleep to be able to work as hard as we do. The trip to and from town takes so long, especially if the wagon is heavily loaded, that getting everything we will need for the winter is a slow process. We work from dawn

     Rita L. McWhorter

to dark, happy and pleased with the progress we are making.

Stanislaus has been a big help to us. Whenever Gregor needs another strong arm, his brother is always there. He brings us fresh vegetables and even chicken and meat. He seldom talks directly to me. So when he drove up in his wagon one day while Gregor was in the hay field, I was surprised to see him. He took off his hat, nodded to me and spoke to Roman and Paul.

"Boys," he said, "ask your mama if she would like to come with us to pick some vegetables. Stella can come, too." At first I hesitated, but the boys insisted, so we got into the wagon. His place is only a couple of miles from ours, so we were there in no time.

First he showed us his huge garden. "I have enough food here for two or three families," he said proudly. "I take things to town to trade for what I need, and give away what I can't eat myself. When I heard you were coming so late in the summer I knew you wouldn't have time to grow your own garden, so this year I planted for your family. Potatoes, see that big patch? Cabbage: enough kraut for everyone! Carrots, turnips, parsnips, too, for winter soup."

He had built a sod cellar. It was like a small house, except he had dug into the ground about two feet before he built the walls. Two wooden steps were planted into the ground leading down to the heavy door. He showed us bins for keeping the root vegetables covered with dirt, and safe from freezing throughout the winter. Bacon and ham were hanging from the ceiling, smoked in a little shack out back. He unhooked a ham and took it with us.

When we went out, the boys wanted to climb the crude ladder that leaned against the side of the cellar. Stanislaus thought it wasn't safe. "But I saw a cat up there," Paul insisted. "Maybe she has kittens. We need a kitten, don't we, Mama?" I agreed. What else could I say?

"Well, you're right. There are kittens up there. I'll hold the ladder. Don't forget, though, you will have to take care of it yourselves."

Just what we need, I thought. A kitten for me to care for. The boys love it. They let Stella pet it. They let me hold it. So small. Soft. Adorable.

I hoped Stanislaus wouldn't ask us into his house; he must have read my thoughts. He hurried us back to the garden. "My house is not for women and children," he explained. "An old bachelor and his dog are not good housekeepers."

He gave us a basket and invited us to pick tomatoes and green beans as he pulled up onions and carrots. We loaded everything into the wagon and started for home. Paul held the kitten, so Roman got to drive the horses. Stella and I sat on the floor guarding the ham and the basket. Stanislaus seemed relaxed, almost jolly as he joked with the boys.

When he brought the basket into the house, I put out some bread and cheese to eat. He said no, he had to go. Silently he shrugged, pushed away our thanks with a shake of his head, and left. The children ran outside, waving and shouting their goodbyes.

Marianna has known Stanislaus a lot longer than I have. Maybe I'll talk to her.

September 5, 1886, Sunday:
Rosie's birthday was yesterday. She is nine years old now, a very grown-up nine-year-old. Marianna baked a cake for her and asked us over to share it after church this afternoon. I envy Marianna's skill with the stove. My

     Rita L. McWhorter

stove is just like hers, and I like cooking on it; using the oven is another matter. Everyone says my bread is very good, but no matter how careful I am to wash my hands after I add chips to the stove, to me it tastes of manure. That thought I keep to myself. No sense putting ideas into other heads.

I will never get used to gathering the chips. The boys hate it too, and I have to be firm with them to get them to help. We go out with Stella and the wheelbarrow, further and further from the house to find buffalo chips. Now that we have cows of our own, we go there first to pick up the dry ones. The rest we flip over with a stick so they will dry out faster. If this is one of the secrets of the prairie Marianna told me about, it is one I wish I didn't have to share.

Today after Mass the organist, Lillian Pitrowski, introduced herself to me. She said she heard I had a good singing voice and had directed the choir back home. "I have been hoping for a choir here at St. Joseph's. Would you be interested in organizing one?"

After I explained that we had been here only a month, and how far away we live, she realized it was too soon for that hope. She was not discouraged. "Maybe you can just sit with me and sing along for now. Do you have a few moments to try a hymn or two?" I looked at Gregor. Stella's hand was in his before I said a word.

What a joy to sing with her! Our voices blend perfectly. We sang both in Polish and in Latin, sometimes together, sometimes in harmony. When it was time to leave, I was surprised to see Gregor rise from a bench in the back of the church. He shook hands with Lillian and told us how much he enjoyed the concert. Then he gathered up our sleepy little daughter and we started for home.

Paul took the reins of our two gentle plodders as they pulled the wagon along the rutted trail. The rest of us sat on the mattresses we had brought with us for the children to nap on.

"I have been thinking we need a buggy and some faster horses," Gregor said. The conversation took off like a spark on dry prairie hay. What kind of buggy? What kind of horses? Mules run really fast, don't they?

"We could go buy them tomorrow, Papa. I can drive these old slow ones home with the wagon. You can drive the new team and the buggy. Roman can stay home and do the chores."

The conversation flared up with that suggestion, but Gregor laughed and calmed it down. He is so good with the boys. And so good to me. It would be a blessing to be able to get to church faster. Maybe we could go more often, too. But I fear we will have to wait awhile for fast horses and a buggy. We need to see if we can get ourselves through the winter before we get more mouths to feed.

The boys asked if we could stop by to see the Dlugoshes. Good idea, I thought, since I wanted to check on Franceska. The last time I saw her she told me she figured her baby was due in February or March. With Joe just a toddler she will have her hands full.

     Rita L. McWhorter

CHAPTER 10

More Land

Sept. 12, 1886:

Sunday afternoon. I have learned something new about my husband. Maybe it is new even to him. He was always a hard worker when we ran the tavern, but here he shows what I call a passion for working the land. He asks his brothers and the neighbors endless questions, drives himself hard, and plans, plans, plans. And whenever he is working he is either concentrating in silence, or he whistles or sings.

Fritz has told him about a government law called the Tree Claim Act and Gregor is all excited about it. To do what the law requires, Gregor must go to our county land office in O'Neill, sign papers for the quarter section of land south of our homestead, and agree to plant trees there for our own use. Then he has to fill out a second set of papers in another county. The nearest county is Knox and the town is Niobrara. After 30 days he must advertise in a newspaper, and wait another 30 days. This is all to make sure no one else has filed a claim for that land. If no one disputes the claims, the land is his and we will get trees to plant.

Niobrara is much further north and east of O'Neill, probably almost 40 miles more if you could go straight for it. But Fritz says it is a long, hard trip with nothing more

JOHANNA   61

than rough trails most of the way. He would go along with Gregor, but he is working on their new house to get the outside finished enough so he can do inside work this winter.

"Don't worry," Gregor says. "I'll figure out some way to get there if I have to walk."

Sept. 17, 1886, Friday:
When Stanislaus heard about the Niobrara trip Sunday afternoon, he said it was too dangerous for Gregor to go alone. "We'll take my team and wagon, so Johanna won't be stuck here alone with no way to get around." Those were his words, according to Gregor. I was surprised and pleased someone was thinking of me in all the excitement of planning the trip. I am not looking forward to being left alone out here.

Today they loaded the wagon with supplies enough for more than two weeks, although they hope the good weather will hold and they won't be gone that long. We stood together just before they left, and Gregor put his arm across my shoulders. He looked serious as he spoke to the boys. "Your mother will be both Mama and Papa while I am gone. I want you both to do what she says, and help her all you can. Be good. Take care of your little sister. Don't fight!" Just as we were all beginning to feel sad with their going, Gregor smiled, leaped into the wagon with Stanislaus, laughing and waving as they drove away. Even Shep (Stanislaus's dog) seemed happy to be part of the adventure.

It is dark now. The children are sleeping and the house is too quiet. Usually at this time of the evening Gregor and I talk together about our day and make plans for tomorrow. I miss him already. This is the first time since we were married six years ago that we have been apart.

          Rita L. McWhorter

I should get ready for bed, but I feel the need to go outside to have a look around. It is a lovely, clear night with stars bright and thick filling the sky. I wonder if Gregor is looking at these same stars now. The air smells sweet, and only the faintest breeze stirs the grass in the fields that stretch all around. The silence is complete but for a small insect softly singing. I can hear a coyote howling far, far off in the sandhills. I feel too small and too alone, so I quickly close the door and listen to the sound of my children's warm breathing.

Sept. 26, Sunday:
Gregor has been gone for nine days now, and I am lonely for him. Even though I am always very tired at night, I don't sleep well. Our bed seems empty and cold. Sometimes the kitten comes to me, but she is usually with Paul. I think we should get a dog. The gun we have might protect us, but I don't really like guns except for shooting wild game for food. Yes, a dog would be good company.

When the weather is good the children and I go out with the wheelbarrow to gather chips for our daily fire and to store up for the winter. Gregor built a shed for wood with a big bin in one corner for the chips and another for dry grass that we twist into tight bundles to burn. The slough grass that grows in the wet places is the best. It is slippery to work with when it is green, but it is thick and lasts longer than prairie grass when it is dry. The men gather wood whenever they are near the river. We are trying to fill the shed before the weather turns cold.

Roman is my big, strong man. He milks the cow morning and night. Paul carries all the water for the house, and between them they do a good job of taking care of the animals. Stella is our little clown and keeps us laughing.

There has been a lot of rain this last week. The house seems small and crowded when the rain keeps pouring down. No leaks yet! Travel must be very hard for the men. There are many rivers and creeks where they are, and they could get stuck in the mud. The rain makes it hard to keep the children occupied. We have been saving the heavy paper we sometimes get from things we buy at the store. One afternoon we cut the paper into squares and drew pictures on them for a game the children play together. Sometimes I play, too, to pass the time in the evening.

This morning the children knelt with me to pray for the safe return of their father and uncle. "And Shep," Roman added.

Oct. 3, Sunday:
Another week has gone by without Gregor. It is nearly three weeks since he left, and I am getting seriously worried. If only there were some way to get news of him and Stanislaus. It has stopped raining and turned cold. I know the men took warm clothes, but it is much colder to sleep outside all night than here in our cozy house. Marianna knows I am worried. She came over one afternoon last week with some of the children and brought rose hips for tea. The children enjoyed the company, and it was a life saver for me to have someone to talk to. Of course, I told her my worries, even though I tried to talk about other things. She said to me, "It's only natural for you be worried and need someone to talk to. Believe me, I understand."

This morning it was still dark when I first looked outside, and also quite cold. We had to wrestle a big box out of a stack of other stored things to get some of our winter clothes. When we opened the door we were greeted by a beautiful

        Rita L. McWhorter

surprise. There was frost on everything in sight. The early morning sun poured over the prairie, setting every blade of grass to sparkling like diamonds. We stopped, huddling together, to gaze at the wonder before us. The kitten changed our mood to laughter. She didn't know what to think of all this cold white stuff. It was a new experience for her, too.

Fritz and Marianna stopped by with the children on their way home from church in the afternoon. They brought some supplies for us, and visited with me while the children played. I was glad to see them and felt a little better when Fritz told me it took him over two weeks to make the trip the last time he went to Niobrara.

"At least the weather was good the first week, and it didn't get cold until last night. They both got plenty of experience camping out when they were in the army. You'll see. They'll show up any day now in good shape."

Oct. 7 Thursday:
Thank God our prayers are answered! Our weary travelers finally came home last night, but I knew as soon as I saw them something was wrong. To start with, Stanislaus had to help Gregor out of the wagon. And when Gregor limped in on crutches, I could tell he was in great pain. The children woke up, of course. We were so upset to see Gregor's foot in a big bandage we all started to ask questions at once and no answers were possible. Gregor sat down and asked for quiet.

"Now, now, too many questions," he said. "I am glad to be home, and happy to see you. Yes, I have a hurt foot; just a little accident. The doctor had a look at it and I'll be better after a good night's rest. Let's just all go to bed now. Tomorrow after morning chores I will tell you the whole story of my trip."

He asked me for some water and took the medicine the doctor had given him. I helped him to bed, and put a pillow under his foot. No, he said. I tried to put the pillow under his head. He shook his head to say no. I felt so sorry he was hurt, but couldn't think any way to help. So I lay down quietly, grateful to have my husband home where at least I could try to take care of him.

October 8, Friday:
Gregor finally got to sleep and stayed in bed later than usual. I knew when he wasn't up at dawn that he had to be feeling really bad. Now he sat in his chair, his foot up on a wooden box. The children sat on the floor, all ears. They had waited a long time to hear this story from their favorite storyteller. I will try to write it down just as he told it.

"On the way to O'Neill the first day we had a little bad luck. I had suggested to Stanislaus that he tie a rope to Shep, but he said, 'Oh, no, he is a good dog. He stays close by me unless I command him to go.' Well, a big jackrabbit came out of nowhere, and ran across the road right in front of the team. The horses shied and went tearing off the road and out across the prairie like they would never stop. Shep jumped out of the wagon and took off after the rabbit. I looked at Stanislaus and asked, 'Did you command Shep to go after that rabbit just now?' He didn't think that was very funny."

The boys thought it was hilarious. Gregor took a few bites of the meal I had put before him while the questions flew. "Did the wagon get stuck?" "Did you break a wheel?" "Did Shep catch the rabbit?"

"We hit some good hard bumps, but nothing broke, thank God. We made it back to the road all right, and Stanislaus whistled for the dog to come back. When Shep appeared he had the biggest rabbit I ever saw. It was a bloody, sandy mess and I wanted to throw it away, but Stanislaus wouldn't let me. He said Shep would be disappointed if we didn't keep it. I'll tell you a secret. When the dog went to sleep I threw the rabbit into the ditch." More laughter and another few bites.

"All that fooling around made us late getting into O'Neill and the Court House office was closed. We drove out of town and fixed our supper over a little fire. When it got dark we sat for awhile, looking at the beautiful sky full of stars. If I'd had my accordion I would have played a sad song, because I was wishing to be home with all of you." He put his hand on mine for a moment and then tousled the boys' hair. Stella climbed into his lap.

"We weren't sure the Court House would be open on Saturday but it was, and I filed for our Tree Claim. While he was waiting for me Stanislaus talked to a Polish fellow who lived north of town. He got some good directions on going to Niobrara that helped us out.

"It was good weather all the way. The road was really more of a trail, but we could see it plain enough, and we had no trouble at all. That whole trip on the way to Niobrara we didn't meet a soul until we were nearly there. We met a young Indian riding a horse. He was wearing regular clothes and a hat like anybody else around here. I did notice, though, he had long, straight black hair hanging down from under his hat, and his skin was a little darker than ours. He spoke to us and seemed friendly, but just rode on past. We got to Niobrara in three or four days, and on Wednesday the 22nd I filed the papers for our Tree Claim.

"I was tired of being on the road so I asked a man there at the Court House who spoke a little Polish where I might find a room to rent for the night. He directed me to a place just down the street that also served home-cooked meals for only a couple of dollars. Of course, Stanislaus didn't want to stay there, but I did. It wasn't like home, but it was better than your uncle's cooking and a hard bed on the ground.

"Niobrara is a nice little town. The name is a Ponca Indian word for 'running water,' the same name as the river that runs by there and flows into the Missouri River. We got a look at the Missouri River. It's pretty wide, but kind of muddy and slow. We heard about some fellows from the East named Lewis and Clark who worked for the Government years ago. They traveled all the way to the Pacific Ocean, measuring the land and making maps. On their way back they came down the Missouri River right past Niobrara when nobody lived here but the Indians. There used to be trouble between the Indians and the settlers, but now everybody seems to get along all right.

"It's pretty country around there, lots of hills thick with trees that were turning bright fall colors. But the town has had its problems. One spring about five years back the Niobrara flooded real bad, and they had to move the whole town to higher ground. They're doing well now, even have a new schoolhouse. I bought a few little things for you. Roman, bring me that satchel there, will you?"

This was just like Gregor, to bring something home for the boys and Stella. Just little trinkets and some candy, but things treasured far beyond their cost. He sipped his coffee as he went on.

"It started to rain the next day. That slowed us down, but it wasn't bad at first. Then the rain got serious. We had trouble staying on the trail. I had laid out our course with my compass on the way up, wrote it down, too, so we

     Rita L. McWhorter

always got back on the right track, but it was hard going. Then we came to a creek that was just a trickle on the way there. Now it was too high to cross. So we followed it one whole day and then some before we figured we could cross. And by golly we did make it across. But the mud was bad on the other side, and we mired down so deep I wondered if we could ever get out. We unhitched the team and tied them to a tree – lots of trees growing there. We gathered up all the big branches we could, and built sort of a bridge out in front of the wagon and in front of the back wheels. Stanislaus brought the team back, slow and patient and we hooked them back up to the wagon. Then he started them up, driving them hard and strong at first, then faster and faster while he thwacked them with the reins, and hollered and yelled encouragement to them. The horses dug in and pulled that wagon right up out of the mud onto hard ground. Stanislaus knew just what he was doing. It was like he had done it a hundred times before. I don't know, maybe he had."

"We were ready to go on toward O'Neill then, but we saw this other wagon coming the same way we had, looking for a way to get across. I waded back across the creek and talked to them. It was a family – Crouch was their name: Heinrich and Anna, and two young children. I told them how we got stuck and pointed over at the branches we had put down. Heinrich listened to every word and answered me in German. Good thing I know a little German! Maybe he knew a little Polish, too. Anyway, Heinrich could see the spot I was talking about and headed straight for it. I walked alongside the wagon just behind the front wheel, ready to push if necessary. We made it across the creek to the mud and were doing all right until the back wheel started to slip off the branches. I was just in front of the back wheel by then, pushing the wagon forward as hard as I could when I slipped and my foot went down into the mud. The wagon was moving fast by then, so I can't be sure exactly what happened, but I think the wheel ran over my foot. The mud and my boot saved me from worse, but my right foot is mighty sore." The room was quiet while Gregor ate the last few bites left on his plate.

"The woman, Anna, wanted me to take off my boot so she could take a look at my foot, but I got stubborn and told her it would be all right. We should learn to listen to the women, boys. Sometimes they know more than we like to admit. The family said goodbye and went off to their homestead, and we drove on to O'Neill. Nice family. Maybe we'll run into them some day."

"I thought seriously about spending that night at the hotel in O'Neill." He took a sip of his coffee.

"At the hotel?" "Did you sleep on a real bed?" "And eat in a fancy dining room?" Where do kids get all these questions?

"No, I decided to go see the doctor instead. He said I probably had a crack in a little bone in my foot and it was bruised pretty bad. Then I had to go to the store and buy some new boots. Because, do you know what that doctor did? He couldn't get my boot off because my foot was swollen, so he grabbed his knife and cut that boot right off and threw it away. My favorite pair of boots, too. But he gave me something instead. Crutches! I'll have to use them to walk with until my foot is well enough to wear my boot."

"That's the end of the story. We made it safely back, that's what counts, so the story has a happy ending. Oh, but wait. I nearly forgot. I got something for Mama, too." It was a small piece of wood, smooth on one side with a picture

     Rita L. McWhorter

of a meadow lark on it. "Painted by hand," he assured me. Welcome home, my dear, dear husband.

October 10, Sunday:
Now I have a stranger in my house. He grumps around, cursing the crutches, complaining about how he can't do this and can't do that. I'll be glad when I have my sweet-tempered Gregor back again.

CHAPTER 11

Holidays

Oct. 17, Sunday:

Fritz and Marianna stopped for a minute early this morning on their way to church. They picked up the papers Gregor had for the tree claim to be published in the paper. Everyone in Atkinson knows Fritz, and that Gregor is his brother, so there will be no problem. It gave me a chance to give them a short list of things I need quite badly. I had to be very stern in order to convince them to take money for the newspaper and the things from the store. I think their hearts are bigger than their pocketbooks.

Nov. 7, Sunday:

There doesn't seem to be even a little corner where I can be alone to write. For some reason, the children think that if Gregor is underfoot, they should be, too, all looking to me for this or that. And too often bickering or quarrelsome.

Gregor's foot was much worse than he thought it would be. In the first couple of weeks unless he kept his foot propped up high, it became swollen and very painful. How he cursed that stupid foot! Finally I became angry myself. I thought, "Are you sure it's the foot that is stupid? Maybe you should look for stupidity at the one using the foul language in front of the children." I became so exasperated that, without a word, I dug out the tablet we use for making plans and put it on the table in front of him. "Put" is probably not the right word to use. The tablet made a sharp noise when it hit the table. Gregor pouted for the rest of the day, but next morning he got busy thinking about spring plowing, and was soon filling the pages with plans.

Fritz invited Stanislaus and the Dlugosh family to come over to our house. Without telling me! On Sunday two weeks ago they all showed up around noon with enough food to feed an army. I added what I had handy, and made coffee and tea. It was a wonderful meal, everyone talking at once, laughing and happy to see each other. After so many days with only our family in the house it seemed so crowded we could hardly move, but no one cared about that.

We were lucky it was a sunny day, not too cold, so the children could go out to play. In no time Fritz organized a card game. I'll never forget how they got into the game with such male gusto, slapping the winning card down on the table, laughing and joking. It did my heart good to see the men put their worries aside and play a game of cards together.

It was also one of the times I was grateful for the partition in our little house. I sometimes resent the room it takes up, but even the small amount of privacy it offers is precious. We three women made ourselves comfortable for a conversation of our own away from the men. Franceska is well along in her pregnancy now, and needed no prodding to talk about her expected baby. Even though this will be her sixth child, she said she was a bit worried.

"I remember how sick I was on the boat when I first got pregnant. It was quite awhile before I could really eat right. I keep worrying that maybe the baby did not get a good start."

With all the experience Marianna has had with mothers and delivering their babies, she knew just the right questions to ask: Did this baby's progress seem normal? Had Franceska had any problems with any of her other pregnancies?

"There was Anna's bad foot, of course, but that had nothing to do with my pregnancy," Franceska noted, "and all the deliveries were normal." Marianna promised to examine her when the birth time came closer. She patted her hand and assured her everything would be fine. What more could we do to calm her fears? Out here, far away from our own families, we have no one to rely upon except each other. We talked on and on, as easily together as though we had known each other for years instead of only a few months.

Too soon the children came bursting into the house. Even though we weren't ready for the afternoon to end, the autumn sun was low and it was time to think of evening chores. Rosie took charge of the children, dipping a small amount of water for whoever was thirsty, and passing around the leftover food.

When the goodbyes were over, company gone, the house became quiet and a little sad. As I made ready to go outside with the boys, Gregor picked up his crutches. "What do you think boys? Can we manage the chores without Mama?"

"Bless you, Fritz," I thought. "Who else would have known a card game might be just the right medicine for Gregor." Stella and I did a little dance together before we began to straighten up the house.

Writing now, two weeks after the party, I realize the card game marked a turning point for Gregor. He set to work on the ruined boot with his awl and some heavy thread, and fixed it so he can get it on his injured foot. After a few days

     Rita L. McWhorter

he was able to discard one crutch. Before long he was using only a cane he borrowed from Stanislaus.

November 21, Sunday:
"Stop fussing," Gregor keeps saying, "my foot is as good as new." I wanted him to go back to the doctor, but he won't have anything to do with that idea. Today we were planning to go into town, but the weather is terrible, first raining, then sleeting or snowing and icy. I can't even remember when I was in church last, and I miss it. Besides that, St. Nicholas Day will be here before we know it and I would like to get to the store to pick up a few things for the children. December 6th comes on a Monday this year.

I was hoping we could visit the Dlugosh family today. I keep remembering Franceska's conversation about her concern for the expected baby. She and I have become very close since we met on the ship, and I think she would have said something earlier if she had thought something was not going right. I think she is just feeling nervous about having the baby out here with no doctor, and having to depend on Marianna. After all, she doesn't know Marianna as well as I do. And even though this will be her sixth child, it will be the first time she will be without her mother, her sister, without any family at all to watch the older children and to hold her hand. Next Sunday for sure we must talk together.

Nov. 28, Sunday Afternoon:
I just looked back in my book and discovered we hadn't been to church for two months. No wonder it was so good to be there again and to sing with Lillian. I was surprised with the number of people who told us they had missed us,

and asked Gregor how his foot was coming along. It made us feel we have a lot of friends who care about us.

The store in Atkinson was prepared for our gift buying. When Gregor said Roman was old enough for a small knife, I didn't agree, but Gregor promised to show him how to use it safely. I found a nice one I am sure Roman will like. I bought a wooden puzzle and a small box of colored pencils for Paul, and a little doll for Stella. Then I found some picture books with English words, three slates with chalk, and a small Polish-to-English book for children like the one we have for adults. Also, a deck of cards for Gregor. I spent more than I should have, but we will have many long winter days and evenings to fill in the coming months. Maybe Gregor and I can learn some English words along with the children. Besides, it has been a long time since I spent money on presents, and I enjoyed every minute.

It is a good thing we stopped by to see Franceska. She was even more upset than I thought. Probably too much worrying by herself without someone to talk to. Women usually don't like to talk such things over with their husbands. We had a few minutes alone together, so I asked her if it would be all right if I stayed with her when her time comes.

"Marianna can stop by on her way here to pick me up. Then Joe can take your children to our house. The men can watch them over there as long as necessary."

I thought for a minute she was going to cry, but instead she just grasped my hands tightly in both of hers for a long moment. Then she wiped her hands on her apron and said, "Johanna, have you planned your garden yet?"

"Franceska, it's only November!" The men came back in the house wondering what we were laughing about.

   Rita L. McWhorter

WHILE I WAS SHOPPING I DIDN'T THINK ABOUT WHERE I could hide all the things I bought. It is a problem to hide anything in our small house. Just last week I made some candies and cookies I wanted to save for the holidays. I put them in a tin box and hid it in the woodshed. I keep checking to see that it is still there, fearing some animal (or some child!) will discover it. But this is too large a package to hide in the shed. Then I remembered that Stanislaus could keep it for us. So I made up a story to use, and we stopped there on our way home. Stanislaus entered into the spirit right away, and promised to keep the "holiday ham" I had bought until we needed it. He told Gregor he would bring it over on Sunday.

Dec. 6, St. Nicholas Day:
Yesterday all the children could talk about was St. Nicholas Day. They had been talking about it for weeks, and the tension was growing. That evening after supper we heard a noise outside, and the door to the shed banged twice. Then there was a scratching at the window. Suddenly the door flew open and a bundle of switches flew into the room. The door banged shut. The children were terrified, especially Stella.

"Those men," I thought. "They never seem to realize how serious a prank like that is to the children. I'll be lucky if they go to sleep at all tonight."

The boys could remember a similar occasion from the year before. They kept reassuring their crying little sister, "Stella, the switches are just a reminder to be good. You have been good, so don't worry. St. Nicholas will surely put something nice in your boots." At bedtime the boys showed

Stella how to put her boots "just so" by the door. It took some calming words, but all three of them finally went to sleep.

Gregor found the package Stanislaus had hidden for us, and my tin of goodies in the woodshed. Together we wrapped the gifts in scraps of paper. We put the small ones into their boots, the others near by, and I blew out the lamp. As usual when I woke up chilly, I rose quietly and put more fuel into the stove. I shushed one small voice by saying, "No, not yet. Go back to sleep." At first light the children were wide awake. What a fuss they made. What a joyous morning!

December 19, Sunday Afternoon:
These last few weeks it has been very interesting to hear the people at church talk about the different ways families celebrated Christmas in the Old Country. In our family, Christmas Eve (Wigilia) was always the most important part of the holiday. We had special food: poppy seed roll, kolaches, cod with gray sauce, wine with dinner, things like that. Then we went to Midnight Mass (Pasterka, or Shepherds Watch). The bells rang out in the cold snowy night, and everyone greeted each other with, "Wesolych Swiat Bozego Narodzenia" (Merry Christmas). The church was always very beautiful with a creche at the side altar, dozens of lighted candles and colorful decorations everywhere. I would direct the choir as we sang the Mass, often with a special guest who played violin, trumpet or accordion. At the finish the congregation would join us as we sang the Polish carols so dear to us all. It was my favorite time of year.

Although there will be a Midnight Mass at St. Joseph's in Atkinson on Christmas Eve, we will not be able to go. It is just too cold to go that far, bumping over the frozen

     Rita L. McWhorter

ground in a wagon late at night. I realized weeks ago that we couldn't go, so I made up my mind that we will just start a few traditions of our own. I will remind the children of some of the traditions we observed in Obrowiec, and write them here so someday perhaps I will be reminded to tell my grandchildren about the old days.

December 25, Christmas Day:
Yesterday, to prepare the table for dinner, I asked Roman to bring a handful of hay from the shed. His face lit up, and as he spread the handful of hay on the table he exclaimed, "I remember! I remember that the hay is in memory of the birth of the Christ Child in the manger. Will we have a candle in the window? And set an extra plate? I remember that we did that, but why did we do it?"

"The candle is in the hope that the Godchild in the form of a stranger might stop by our house this special evening. There is an old adage, "A guest in the home is God in the home."

We spread a cloth over the wisps of hay, and put the dishes out. Using a tablecloth in itself signified a special occasion. Two candles made it even better.

"At home, before sitting down at the table we always shared a special wafer called oplatek that we bought at the store. It is called the bread of love. We will have to make do with the loaf of babka you helped me bake today. We will each take a piece and remember the loved ones who are not with us tonight."

Before the silence became too sad, I served our first course of sardines and crackers. "In olden days dinner might have been a feast with seven, nine or eleven courses, but those days have been gone for a long time. Even in Obrowiec the dinner is not that fancy any longer, but one thing is still the same. Christmas Eve has always been a day of fasting, so no meat is served." I ladled the stew made with milk, potatoes and onions into their bowls.

Dessert was a compote made of dried fruit, a slice of poppy seed roll and special nuts and candies. As we began to clear the table, Roman remembered that in Poland we always sang carols when dinner was over. He began with his favorite. Then we sang another and another until before we knew it, the leftover food was put away, and the dishes were back in the cupboard.

Now it became the time we had all been waiting for. After St. Nicholas Day I had suggested we make gifts for each other. This had taken a lot of thought and some doing, but the presents were wrapped and we were all very curious to see what was in the little packages.

Stella's gifts were more in the "It's the thought that counts" category I had emphasized: scribbles on scraps of paper she folded and then wrapped with other scraps of paper she had scribbled on. But we praised her highly. Paul won the prize for most mysterious. He had made only one gift. We gave Gregor the honor of opening it. It was our old card game, the one we had made on brown paper months ago. He had collected a variety of good quality paper, and used his colored pencils to draw pictures and designs on them. Some even had pictures pasted on their surface. They are certainly something to be proud of.

Roman, of course, had used his most prized possession, his new knife, to make his gifts. He made what he called a paintbrush for Stella, a very smooth stick with the end of it cut into bristles. We'll see just what Stella uses it for. The rest of us got some version of a wooden knife, carefully

    Rita L. McWhorter

whittled, but not sharp. "I didn't want you to hurt your-selves," he explained.

Gregor had to bring his gift in from outside. It is a hat rack to put by the front door, really quite ingenious, since it is impossible to hang anything on a sod house wall. It is meant to stand by itself, but it may require a little more work to make sure it won't fall over.

I made each of them a small pouch with a drawstring at the top. Inside I put a few coins. Paul especially liked the gift. "Now I have a place to keep all my money." He said it as though he had a great pile of money scattered about.

It had been a long, happy day. At last the lights were out, all was quiet and Gregor lay close to me as we talked about the evening. "I worried that you would be too sad to enjoy this Christmas Eve, Johanna. But instead of looking back, you made it a wonderful new beginning for our life here. Wesolych Swiat Bozego Narodzenia, Johanna," he whispered.

Actually, it wasn't nearly as difficult as I had feared it would be. The more I thought about it, the more I believed it was one of the nicest Christmas Eves I'd ever had.

This morning the church looked very festive with many lighted candles and bright decorations. The creche at the side altar was simple and beautiful. Stella couldn't stop look-ing at the tiny baby in the manger. I think the Christmas story we had told her seemed to come alive for her. Later, when the priest read the Christmas story in Polish she looked at me and smiled with delight. It was probably the first time he said anything that interested her.

Lillian played the organ and led us in singing the carols, Polish, English and German. We followed along as best we could with the unfamiliar songs, and sang out loud and clear the ones we knew.

After Mass we shared coffee, pastries and conversation with our friends and neighbors for more than an hour. Happy greetings in several languages filled the room. Fritz and Marianna were there with their family, as well as Frank and Magdelana and many of our neighbors, some of them new to us. I always dread the thought of the long, cold, bumpy ride to church over the frozen ruts in the road, but when I am there I know how important it is to us all. We are too much alone, especially in the winter.

Stanislaus stopped by this afternoon, "For a cup of coffee," he said. We made him sit and filled him up with soup and compote. He loved the babka, so we kept urging him to eat more until he finished the whole loaf.

It's all very different here, but Christmas is still my favorite time of the year.

     Rita L. McWhorter

CHAPTER 12

Happy New Year

January 1, 1887, Saturday:

Happy New Year! Before Christmas, when I realized New Year's Day was on Saturday, I thought we would probably just celebrate at church on Sunday. The more I thought about it the more I missed our parties at the tavern back home. So Gregor and I decided to have a New Year's Eve Party on Friday evening. Gregor and the boys hitched up the team one afternoon and we made the rounds of those close to us. Stanislaus, usually shy about invitations, thought it was a great idea. "I'll bring a ham," he said with a big grin. When Marianna heard about the ham, she said to count on her for bread. Rosie promised cookies. Fritz gave Gregor a wink and said he would think of something. Franceska had poppy seed to make a roll, and we got another sly wink from Joe. It sounded like we would bring the New Year in with good cheer.

Last evening after chores were over, we all put on our best clothes. This was my chance to wear the deep rose blouse I had brought with me. I couldn't bear to leave it home, but I wondered if I would ever get to wear it. And I had a big puffy bow I could stitch onto my good black skirt for the night. Watching me dress, Stella knew something exciting was happening. I helped her put on the red Christmas dress her Grandmother had made. I'm afraid this will be the last time she can wear it, she is getting so big. Maybe I can let it out a little more so she can wear it through the winter.

The boys with their white shirts and slicked down hair fairly glowed. "My feet hurt in these shoes," Paul complained.

"Just keep them on until our company gets here," was Roman's advice. Later you can put on your slippers and nobody will notice."

Gregor was a surprise in a white shirt with big puffy sleeves embroidered in bright colors down the front. It was a shirt he used to wear when he played the accordion for special occasions. I didn't even know he still had that shirt. He also had carefully trimmed his curly red beard and looked very handsome.

Our guests soon filled the house with laughter and good cheer. Except for church we never saw each other in such fine clothes. Rosie appeared in a blue dress with a blue ribbon in her hair. John had a blue shirt and from his grimace I could tell his shoes wouldn't stay on any longer than Paul's. But he gave me a big smile and a hug. The twins were dressed alike in blue the same shade as John's shirt, with big white collars. William wore a shirt just like Joseph's. Frank was already asleep and Marianna put him down on the bed.

"Marianna, you have been sewing, I see," I said. The children all look beautiful. And I love your blouse. Did it come from Poland?"

"Yes, yes." She looked a little tired, but why wouldn't she be tired? "My aunt in Poland sent me this blouse many years ago, and I love having a chance to wear it. Thank goodness

         Rita L. McWhorter

it was a little big when I got it. The color blue has always been my favorite, as you can tell." She laughed and gestured toward all the children dressed in their blue.

Franceska took the prize. Over her usual dress she wore a loose, brightly colored robe that flowed softly around her. Everyone clustered around her, telling her how beautiful she looked. "It's from my marriage clothes," she explained. "I haven't worn it in a very long time."

Stanislaus came, all shined up, wearing trousers and a wrinkled but clean almost white shirt. I didn't know he ever wore anything but overalls. He put the ham down, still warm, neatly sliced and ready to eat. Then he lifted the lid of the stew I had cooked and inhaled loudly.

"Aaah, bigos! That smells like home, Johanna."

We were all in a festive mood, and feasted on bread and ham, and the stew I had cooked with meat and kraut. There was tea and coffee, milk for the children, and babka, poppy seed roll, and apples. As we stood, eating and drinking together the talk got louder and the party got better. When the table was cleared the card game began. The children played together or stood by the table to watch and learn the game the men enjoyed. The men began to get a little wild, what with all the wink, winking going around, and the children were becoming bored. One by one they drifted to their mothers looking for something else to do.

"Rosie," I said, "it seems to me we have enough for a children's choir. What do you think?"

"Oh, yes! John and Johnny, that's what I call John Dlugosh, Anna, Roman and Paul. Even the little ones can sing some of the songs. What should we sing?" In a minute she had them singing together, and it didn't take long for the women to join in. Soon the cards were forgotten and everyone was singing. Each one had a favorite, and each song reminded us of another. Then Fritz sang about a sailor who did a drunken jig. He didn't have much room to put on his show, but it was hilarious. We all roared with laughter. I had never heard Stanislaus laugh so loud before. If Roman hadn't been watching the time we would have missed the midnight hour. We brought in the new year in fine style, with toasts, kisses and hugs, and fervent wishes for the coming year.

When Franceska said it was time to go home, I tried to convince her to stay a little longer. "No, I have laughed so much, I am afraid I will have the baby right here if I stay any longer. It is time to pack up our sleepy little ones and take them home. Thank goodness we don't have far to go." The children were roused from a soft pile of coats, a comfortable corner or a lap where they had slept until their parents decided it was time to take them to their own beds. They were soon wrapped in the warm quilts and robes and bundled off home.

Goodnight, goodnight. Happy New Year! The voices rang out in the still night, some happy, some sleepy.

Stanislaus was the last to go. For the first time he took my hand in both of his. He thanked me for the wonderful party. He said he could not remember when he had such a good time.

"Wait," I said. "There is bigos left in the pot. Just enough for your dinner tomorrow. Take it, take it!" I easily pushed aside his feeble attempt to decline, and he went away happy. I thought of what Mama often said, something about the way to love is through the stomach.

It is now long after midnight and I am tired, but not sleepy. The family is in bed and the house is quiet. I had

        Rita L. McWhorter

such a good time at the party, but now I sit by myself in my pretty dress, overwhelmed with homesickness. I miss the parties we used to have. Here there is no tavern, no grandma to take care of the children. Not even an accordion to help with the music. I miss my home, my family gathered around the kitchen table for Sunday dinner. Mama, her face flushed from the cooking, Papa looking proud of us all. The friends I went to school with. Usually I push my feelings aside to put on a show of strength and cheerfulness. Tonight I just can't do that. Tonight I weep alone in a small house far away from home on this lonely, bleak prairie.

Jan. 20, Thursday:
We had our first real snowfall two days ago. Poland has plenty of cold and snow, and we all love watching it come down. It is like magic to see the familiar things become hard to recognize in their new blanket of white. This snow started gently in early afternoon, but by the time we had looked after the animals, we were glad to go inside. It had turned colder, the wind had come up and it was no longer fun to be outside.

The next morning it wasn't snowing quite as hard but the wind was fierce. We began to see what the wind can do. Since there are no trees, there is nothing to stop the wind except our house, our shed and the shelter for the animals. In some of the level places the snow was only up to my knees, but the drifts were piled high. It was a good thing we had brought the shovel into the house because we needed it to get into the shed for fuel for the stove. The snow bank there was almost up to Gregor's head. We managed to get out to feed the animals, but the wind never let up.

Today has been beautiful. When Roman and I went out early with water to prime the pump, we heard Marianna's rooster crow in the cold, silent morning. The dawn took my breath away. The world was a fantasy land of white all around us and as far as we could see. As the sun began to rise it spread a rosy glow, then everything began to glisten and sparkle. In the fields the wind had sculpted endless, sweeping patterns outlined by dark shadows where no shadows had existed on the prairie before.

The children rushed through breakfast, eager to try out this wonderful new place to play. The wind had swept the snow from the back of the house and piled it around the east corner into a huge snow bank. The snow was packed so hard we could walk on the surface without breaking through. The children loved it, the biggest hill they had seen since we came here. They climbed up and tried to slide down, to roll down, to run down, laughing with the fun of being free to play outside. They raced to the fields, tramping their footprints into the unbroken snow that seemed to stretch out forever. Stella did her best to keep up but soon came to the door with cold fingers and toes, crying to come in. When the boys finally burst in covered with snow, puffing and blowing they looked half frozen. But as soon as they warmed up they couldn't wait to go out again.

By afternoon the scene had changed to blinding brightness. A quickening breeze turned into a stiff wind that blew icy scraps of snow across the fields like whitecaps atop the unmoving waves that rose above a frozen sea. In late afternoon the calm returned and all became deathly cold and silent once more.

The best thing about helping with evening chores is the sunset. The sun squats on the horizon like an old man,

     Rita L. McWhorter

tired but satisfied that his day's work was well done. When he slips below it is with such a blazing fire that you expect the earth to melt. Then the clouds begin to glow with ever changing colors, sometimes for an hour or more. Tonight, with the contrast of the snow, it was more spectacular than ever. Before it was completely dark we could see the evening star that follows the path of the sun.

Maybe the sunset looks the same in Poland, I don't know. I can't remember that I ever watched the sun go down when I lived there. Out here it is a lovely, silent evening prayer.

CHAPTER 13

A New Life

Feb. 16, Wednesday:

My pleasure with the snow is fast turning to exasperation, just one storm after another since the first one. I wouldn't mind so much if it weren't so close to Franceska's due date. I did manage to get over there one day and found her all right, but fretful. "What if my time comes and there is a blizzard raging outside? I would have to rely on Joe alone."

"No," I told her as firmly as I could. "Don't wait until the last minute to let Marianna know. When the first pains come, you send Joe for Marianna, and for me, too."

Feb. 24, Thursday:

Franceska took my advice and Joe came before light this morning. Marianna was already in the wagon, and when we got back to the Dlugosh house, all the children were dressed and ready to go back to our house. To them it was a holiday, but I wasn't too sure Joe and Gregor would enjoy it all that much.

Marianna and I stayed most of the morning, but after awhile it became apparent that it was a false alarm. After the pains stopped Franceska felt embarrassed. "You would

     Rita L. McWhorter

think that after five children I would know when my time had come," she fussed.

"You do know, Franceska, but the baby doesn't agree with you," Marianna teased. "The baby will come when he or she is ready, and not before. Anyway, we have had a nice visit and no harm done. You did the right thing to send Joe for us when you did. Be sure you do the same thing next time. Get some rest now."

Joe came in the house as we were talking and looked worried when he found out the pains had stopped. That had never happened before in his experience. Marianna assured him it was not unusual, and convinced him it was nothing to be concerned with. By the time we got to our house he was ready to make a little joke to his children when they crowded around him wanting to know if it was a boy or a girl. "I think maybe it is a baby rabbit because it decided to stay hidden. But don't worry, the baby will come another day."

The house looks like the children had a great time playing together. Books, games and toys are scattered everywhere. Most of the dishes are left out, dirty. Everything out of place. Of course the older ones were in and out, tramping snow in the house until the floor is really a mess. Oh well, it will dry out overnight. It's a good time for teaching a lesson to my husband and children on how to entertain company when Mama is not here, and how to clean up after the company is gone.

Feb. 25. Friday:
The sky hung low and grey this morning. "Looks like more snow, boys," Gregor said. How can he stay so cheerful day after day with so much snow and cold? He had the boys

pile extra chips and wood into the house, and prepare for another storm as best we could. By afternoon big white flakes were drifting down. Then the wind picked up. Now, at bedtime, it is another blizzard and the snow is piling up.

Feb. 27, Sunday:
Here I am again on Sunday evening, this time to write about our Saturday night. What a night we had! The wind had been blowing like a wild thing all day, driving the snow across the fields and banking it up into deep drifts against the house. It was just past suppertime and another long, quiet evening stretched before us. The loud knock on the door startled us but we knew it had to be Joe. This time he came stomping in, cursing the snow, with little Joe a bundle of blankets in his arms. Anna led Hedwig by her mittened hand, and John pushed Frank inside while he struggled to close the door.

"It's Franceska. I got Marianna for her this afternoon, and she sent me for you, Johanna. Is it all right if the children spend the night?" Of course it was.

John and Anna went back to the wagon for more blankets, and before Joe and I left Anna, good little mother that she was, already had the smaller children in a circle clapping their hands to the tune of a familiar song.

Joe was relieved to have the children off his hands. He was upset and very worried about Franceska. She had been having pains off and on since early morning, and he thought maybe he should go for the doctor. But with the snow already deep with more coming down, and the wind blowing like the devil he wasn't sure he could even make it to town. So he worried and stewed.

When we got to Franceska we found that her pains had slowed again and she was trying to rest. Marianna was

     Rita L. McWhorter

calm and told Joe she felt sure the time was near, and that everything would be all right. Joe hung around getting in the way until we told him he should stop worrying and go bed down for the night with Gregor and the children. After he left, Marianna confided in me that she was not as sure as she tried to sound. The baby was not positioned for an easy birth, and unless she could turn him we were in for serious trouble. She had delivered a breech birth twice before and was pretty sure she could do it again, but this baby was a big one. It wouldn't be easy. "Still, though, what is the sense of Joe going out in this storm and maybe getting lost and freezing to death, when with God's help we'll be able to bring this baby and Franceska safely through." By midnight the pains had increased and the birthing began.

My place was next to Franceska, to encourage her to do whatever Marianna directed: "Breathe, Franceska, breathe," then "Don't push, don't push. Keep her quiet, Johanna." I talked to her. I sang to her. I held her hand. The pains continued. A cool cloth for her forehead, a sip of water. I stroked her hair. The pains grew worse. Franceska asked for her rosary. "Hail Mary, full of grace..." we prayed, over and over, on and on. How much longer could we pray and wait? Marianna talked quietly to herself as she worked. Louder she said, "Breathe, Franceska, breathe." Finally, the pains grew impossibly strong, "Holy Mary Mother of God," Franceska screamed. Marianna's voice was a command. "Now push, Franceska. That's it, push. That's good! Push hard!"

"I see his head! I see his head! Once more, Franceska. Push! Push!" Franceska grasped my hands as if to wring from me the strength I tried to give her with all my heart. "Here he comes. Oh, thank you, God, thank you. Franceska, it's a boy! You have a big, healthy boy. Thank you, Lord, thank you. Now, Johanna, come help me with the baby." Marianna held him by his feet, as she had been taught and on his own he gave a lusty cry. The three of us joined him, crying and laughing, overjoyed and grateful we had brought him safely into the world.

We worked together, exhausted but elated, until everything had been washed and cleaned. There were fresh linens on the bed and Franceska lay quietly, her new son in a little crib beside her. We helped her take a little broth and some tea and she was soon asleep. Marianna and I were too tired to talk much, but we sat at the table enjoying our rose hip tea. We had come a long way from that summer day when we had our first cup of tea together. It seemed like that was a long time ago.

Joe came before daylight, relieved and pleased to see he had a healthy son and that his wife was sleeping peacefully. Yes, it was a peaceful scene, too peaceful to suit Marianna. She felt Joe needed to understand the difficult time Franceska had been through, lest he treat her condition too lightly.

"She managed to stay pretty strong throughout the birthing, Joe, but it was a long, hard labor. You will need to make sure she gets a few weeks to rest and recover. Don't let her get back to working hard too soon." Joe nodded in agreement. She had never had such pain for so long with any of the others, and he had never been so worried before.

Joe took me home and I insisted he stay for breakfast. Marianna was watching over Franceska and the new baby, and they wouldn't need him for a little while. He stayed to eat, but then hurried off. It was all I could do to convince him the children should stay longer. The children, too, soon wanted to go home to be with their mother and their new

     Rita L. McWhorter

brother. At noon I fixed them something to eat and we drove them home.

We found Joe waiting on Franceska, who was propped up with pillows holding the new baby. Fritz had come earlier and had taken Marianna back home. Joe picked up the baby to show the children their new brother.

"See how big and strong he is, John? We named him Karol. Before we know it he will be helping us in the field, Ja?"

"I don't know, Papa, he looks awful small to me."

"Papa, can I hold him?" Anna could wait no longer. "Oh, look, Hedwig, see his tiny fingers. See Frank? And feel his soft, soft hair."

Little Joe, hardly more than a baby himself, didn't understand what the excitement was all about. He climbed up into Joe's lap and went to sleep.

It is now dark and all is quiet once more. The storm has finally worn itself out, and so have I. Sleep is what I need, but as usual, I cannot rest until I write in my book. It isn't every day I am asked to assist in the birth of a child. I don't think I appreciated before today what a miracle a new life truly is, and I feel honored to have been able to help. Franceska was brave beyond her strength, and if I ever had any doubts about Marianna's midwife skills, they have been completely erased. She did a wonderful job and she did it with compassion and love.

Now I can go to bed – almost. First I must mix up a batch of bread and set it to rise overnight. With all those hungry children in the house, there is not even a crust left for us to eat tomorrow.

CHAPTER 14

The Hope of Spring

March 20, 1887, Sunday Evening:
Roman and I were priming the pump at dawn this morning, talking about how clear and silent it was when we heard Marianna's rooster crow. I said I thought his crow held a note of hope that spring is on its way. The wind was sharp, but the sun rose, bright and brave.

"The ground is still frozen, Mama, and the roads are rutted and rough. Will we go to church?" I told him there was no question about going to church. Today was the day for baby Karol to be christened and we had a special invitation to attend. Franceska told us she had asked the priest if she could have Marianna and me, two godmothers instead of the usual couple, but he said no, he didn't think that would be acceptable. So Marianna and Fritz were chosen Godparents, as seems proper to me. It was a simple and beautiful ceremony, much like the ones performed for our babies in Poland. Neighbors and friends took the place of close families, and the whole congregation offered congratulations and good wishes. Several of the women, including some who barely knew Franceska, gave her baby clothes and toys their children had outgrown. Franceska was so happy!

 Rita L. McWhorter

We are very short of wood to burn so we stopped along the river to see if we could find a few branches to load into the back of the wagon. The hay and straw in the wagon box we used all winter to help keep us warm was pretty worn out, so we pushed it to the front to make room for the wood. We stacked in a good pile, which was surprising because so many people collect those precious sticks.

The willow bushes caught my eye. Even though the little river was still partly covered with ice, the willows showed a tinge of green, and their buds seemed just the tiniest bit swollen. Gregor laughed when he heard me showing the children.

"You have sharp eyes, Johanna, and if you keep looking for those small signs of spring, soon we'll all be able to see them." I guess there is a bit of wishing in my observations, but I am weary of winter to my very bones.

Joe Dlugosh had said he wanted to talk to Gregor, so we stopped by on the way home. Joe had never done any farming so he had a lot of questions. I overheard some of their conversation.

Gregor said, "We never owned land in Poland, but I worked on the farms nearby. It's hard work. Still, I never found anything else I would rather do. There is a lot of satisfaction in seeing what you do with your hands become the food you put on the table. I have to admit, though, before we came I worried about farming in another country. How would we know which was the crop and which were the weeds? What would we plant? But just looking at the fields last fall, I saw that it's not so different. You'll find out you know a lot more than you think.

"The weather seems to be harder to learn. At home I could tell at a glance at the sky if it would be a good planting day or a good drying day, whether it might rain or snow. But that's not easy for me now. Even the clouds here look different. It's all before us to experience and learn. Mostly the hard way, I guess," he laughed.

"That seems to be the way it goes most of the time, we have to learn the hard way," Joe nodded. "There's one thing we know very well, though. There are good people here. Neighbors become friends." He looked at Franceska who was nursing the baby. "We'll never forget how much you helped us, and if you or Johanna ever need us, we'll always be willing to help out." Feeling awkward, both men stood up and shook hands heartily, pounding each other on their backs. Gregor cleared his throat. "Get your coats everybody. Time to go home."

As I write this evening my spirits are high. It did me good to go to church, and to visit with neighbors and friends. And seeing the new baby made me realize how much my own baby Stella has grown. It doesn't seem possible that she will be two years old in April. She is such a sweet little thing, really no trouble at all, uses her little pottie and seldom has an accident. She is mama's little helper. Give her a pan of water and something to wash, and you couldn't ask for a happier child. Her imagination never quits and she is a delight to us all. She listens to every word we say, and you never know what will come out of her mouth next.

The boys have grown, too, and our new life has changed them. Changed us all, I guess. We have spent the winter here in this little house, cozy and warm, yes, but too much together. We seldom see our neighbors, and when the weather is bad we are stuck inside with only small snatches of time away from each other. I teach the children stories from the Bible and we are learning a little English together,

    Rita L. McWhorter

but we never know if we are pronouncing the words cor-
rectly. The boys get bored without friends to play with and
that leads to squabbles and tears. Sometimes they get so
angry they start to fight and I am afraid they will hurt each
other or knock over a lamp or something. When things get
that bad, Gregor orders the boys to sit down on the floor
near the stove. He brings his chair up, holds Stella on his
lap and helps us dream of the future.

"Next summer we will build a great barn, all the neighbors will help. It will have stalls for the horses and a place
for the cows. And it will have an upstairs, with a ladder to
climb to get up there. When it is finished we will have a huge
celebration, a barn dance! Everyone invited. Fiddlers will
play, and if somebody brings an accordion, I will borrow it
and play a little myself. Yes, and sing and dance."

"The barn will be so big you can go out and play in it
on dark snowy or rainy days. We will have hay stored up in
the hay mow for you to jump on. Down below there will be
stalls for the horses, and room for the cows and baby calves,"
and so he goes, on and on.

It is not an easy life, but we are lucky to have each
other and these three healthy, happy children. I haven't
said anything to Gregor, but I have missed my period so I
think I am probably pregnant. Having just gone through
the birthing with Franceska I admit I have mixed feelings.
It isn't that I don't want another baby. It's just that we are so
alone out here, and in bad weather there may be nowhere
to turn for help. But I have strong faith in Marianna, and
when I hold little Karol I am reminded of the joy of having
a new baby, God's most precious gift. We will just have to
pray, and hope for the best.

March 27, Sunday:
Stanislaus came over during the week with his wagon filled with trees to be planted in the Tree Claim. He said he was in town and heard they were there, so he got then loaded up and brought them out. The ground is still frozen but the men took Roman and Paul to help and they unloaded the trees. It won't be long before we can get them in the ground. Some day that quarter section of land will be ours. It is still hard for us to believe that we will actually own this huge piece of land just by planting some trees on it.

Looking back in my book I realize I didn't remark that February 23 was Ash Wednesday. We couldn't go to church, but we did start the Lenten season, following the usual fasting customs of less meat and smaller meals. There is not much we can give up as a meaningful sacrifice, since we have very little in the way of sweets or spirits, so we decided we would pray together more often instead. If you could see Paul squirming and Stella trying to be quiet while we say the Rosary on Wednesday evenings, you would realize it is quite a sacrifice for them. Roman, though, is serious about it, and even reminds us if he thinks we might forget. On Sundays when we can't get to church we read the bible and talk about the life and death of Jesus. It has been a religious experience for the whole family, and we're all looking forward to Easter.

CHAPTER 15

Easter Sunday

April 11, 1887:

It is unusual for me to write on Monday evening, but yesterday was Easter Sunday, and we had a very long day. Let me explain:

Sometime early in Lent Father Engelbrecht announced that *Swieconka*, or the blessing of Easter baskets, would take place after Mass on Easter Sunday instead of having it the customary way on Holy Saturday. Those of us who live so far away were very happy to hear about that.

The baskets usually contain ham, bread, sausage, salt, pepper, eggs, and butter formed in the shape of a lamb as a symbol of Christ, and everyone bakes special breads and cakes. All are covered by our best and prettiest linen cloths. Most people decorate their boiled eggs with colors and designs, sometimes very ornate. This is an important custom in Poland, and we are all looking forward to it.

Thinking I might get Stanislaus interested in coming to church with us, I asked him to bring the ham for the basket. He came in with it on Saturday when we were getting ready to color and decorate the eggs. To my surprise he began to help, remembering things he and his family used when they were children, such as onion skins for yellow, and beet juice for red. I had baking to do, so I just kept out of the way. It did my heart good to see the four of them working so happily together.

When Gregor came in at noon for dinner the table was covered with beautiful eggs for our admiration. We ate our soup standing up while we looked and listened to stories of other Easter Saturdays when the brothers had dyed Easter eggs in their kitchen at home.

Suddenly Stanislaus became very quiet. "I will be here in the morning to drive you all to church," he announced. Without another word he stomped out and closed the door. We were left speechless.

Finally Gregor said, "I never thought I would hear those words from him."

Stanislaus was not known for going to church. He said it made him too homesick. I didn't say it aloud, but I wasn't sure if we could count on him, or if he would actually go into the church. After all he only said he would drive us to church. Would he really come inside with us?

True to his word, Stanislaus was here early the next morning, and I has glad to see he was dressed for church. We had all put our dark winter clothes aside, and wore the finest spring clothes we had. At least the children had new clothes. Even Paul. I had thought he could wear Roman's things as Roman outgrew them, but they just don't fit him.

The two men sat on the seat while the children and I snuggled together on the clean hay in our corner of the wagon. It was too muddy for Shep to run alongside the wagon, so he pushed his way in to the middle of our circle, and it was all the boys could do to keep him away from our big Easter basket. The sun was in and out of clouds left over from yesterday's rain. I was hoping the sun would win.

     Rita L. McWhorter

By the time we reached town, wagons and buggies were everywhere, coming together for this wonderful celebration of the Resurrection. I needn't have wondered about Stanislaus; he had no choice. The children jostled for the privilege of holding his hands, and walked him straight into the crowded church. One family made room for Stella and me, Gregor managed to seat the two boys, and he and Stanislaus joined several men already standing in the back. The church was beautifully decorated with tree branches, some with early blossoms, and bright colors were everywhere. Especially the hats. I felt out of place wearing last year's poor excuse for a proper hat, but I soon forgot about myself. Just as at home, all the somber draperies of the Lenten season were gone. The garments of the priest and his servers were white and gold and the spirit of Easter was everywhere.

Lillian had asked me to sing the hymn at Communion. I felt honored to sing with her accompaniment at the organ, but a little nervous. We had not rehearsed together and I could hear Mama saying, "Practice doth the master make." So, imagining myself with my choir back home, I sang with them, and it was fine.

The blessing of the baskets was followed by a joyous gathering in the Parish Hall. We all shared the food from our overflowing baskets, sampling new treats and getting better acquainted with the people who had brought them. What satisfied my hunger the most was the talk and laughter, the close companionship of these warm, generous people who were becoming our friends.

Gregor and the children were having the same experience but Stanislaus was no longer in the room. "This was just too much for him," I thought. "But he will be around when it is time to go home."

I was wrong. Just as we were leaving church a loud clap of thunder announced a lightning strike that seemed to shake the church. "That was close," somebody said. The wind came sweeping in, dark clouds crowded in from the west and plump drops of rain were already falling on the ground. The church emptied quickly. Men rushed to ready their teams while mothers, holding onto their new Easter hats, hurried their children to their wagons and buggies before the storm arrived. In only minutes there was not a single horse or a wagon in sight. We were left shivering and looking up and down the street for Stanislaus. I couldn't believe he would abandon us. Was all this thinking of home too much for him? Was he sick? Did the team panic and run away? Was he hurt? How would we get home? Would we be stranded here for the rest of the day? For the night? Where could he be?

Just then the church door opened and the priest came out.

"Hurry, hurry," he said as he held the door for us. "You can wait in here. Where is your wagon?"

Gregor explained we had come with Stanislaus. "Shortly before the rest of us were preparing to leave, Stanislaus went out. I figured that he went to get the mules hitched up when the storm came. He gets very upset when there is thunder. He thinks it is the sound of the guns in the war, and often gets a terrible headache. But the team might have been frightened and run away. I will have to go look for him."

"Can I go with you?" Roman wanted to know.

Gregor looked at me and I nodded my head in approval. "Yes, that's probably a good idea," he said "We might need another hand when we find the wagon." Then seeing the disappointment on Paul's face, he took him gently by the shoulders and spoke softly to him.

     Rita L. McWhorter

"Sometimes a man has to stay with those who need him the most. This time it is you who has to stay to watch out for your mother and your sister. Can you do that for me?" Paul wasn't too happy, but he dutifully nodded and took Stella's hand.

We followed Father Engelbrecht back to the room that had just been packed with happy people. It was deserted now and very quiet. Before I could think what to do next the room became dim and gloomy with another thunder shower crashing down. Stella began to cry. As I comforted her, worries filled my mind, building to the unreal exaggeration of spending the night here in the empty church basement. Finally she fell asleep. Searching my mind for something to do to pass the time, I realized Father had already solved the problem. He had found a deck of cards and he and Paul were enjoying a game together.

Stella was awakened by another clap of thunder, but we were soon learning yet another card game and munching a snack from the Easter basket. But the time began to drag and we began to wonder if our men would ever come back.

When we heard Roman announce they were back, Father confided that it was a good thing they finally got back. "I was running out of games to teach Paul. The next one was going to have to be poker." That surprised me and we had a good laugh as I thanked him as sincerely for giving us a safe place and for entertaining us so well.

The sun was getting low in the sky, but at least the storm was over, and the hay in the wagon had begun to dry. Shep lay next to Stanislaus who was sleeping restlessly on a pile of feed sacks covered by a blanket in the back of the wagon. Gregor looked tired. He took a long drink from the water jug. "Paul, look in the basket. Did you hungry boys leave anything for me to eat?" Roman took the reins and we headed for home. Gregor ate some bread and ham and began to tell us about finding Stanislaus.

"Often when Stanislaus comes to town he leaves the mules at the stables by the train depot, so we went there first. Tom and Elizabeth Owings run the business, and they live in the house there with their son Joe. They hadn't seen Stanislaus, so Joe hitched a horse to the buggy and we drove around to see if he was still in town. No one had seen him so I figured the mules had headed for home, and Joe took the road we always use. When we got to the place where that big pig pen is alongside the road, just before it takes a sharp turn to the south, we had a bit of good luck."

"It was Shep," Roman couldn't wait to describe the scene. "Good old Shep was barking his head off," he gushed, "and we got out of the buggy, and Shep came running and jumping through some brush and weeds over to us, all excited, and that was when we saw the wagon."

Gregor explained that the mules must have been out of control and couldn't make the turn. Instead they went off into a field and down into an overgrown gully. Anyone coming along the road wouldn't see the wagon, and would just go on around the corner. "We probably would have gone right past if we hadn't heard the dog barking."

"When went down to the wagon it looked as though the front wheel had hit a stump, the mules broke loose, the wagon tipped and Stanislaus fell out. He bumped his head on something and passed out. When he came to, he could feel a bump above his left eye and there was blood everywhere. He used his shirt to stop the bleeding from a cut near the bump and crawled under the wagon to get out of the rain. That's where we found him."

          Rita L. McWhorter

"That nice white shirt he wore to church?" I couldn't help asking.

"Yes, well he didn't have anything else he could use."

"Did the mules run off? Maybe they ran all the way home," Paul observed.

"No they were grazing in the field nearby, calm as could be."

"Why didn't Shep go for help?" Paul asked Roman.

"He knew Uncle Stanislaus was hurt. Shep is a good dog and he would never leave his master's side, if he was hurt. But I think he heard our voices and that's why he came running up to us," Roman said. "We should get a dog like Shep, Mama." Paul agreed with him and I had some trouble getting Gregor back to telling the story.

"Was the wagon badly damaged?" I asked.

"No, thank God. It could have had a broken wheel, but we were lucky. The mules' harness was torn up pretty bad, though. Joe had brought some wire and other gear so we managed to patch things up pretty well. Between the three of us we got the wagon straightened out and the mules hitched up again. The hardest part was getting the wagon out of that gully, but we made it all right. I think our horses would have had a harder time; those mules are really a fine team. Stanislaus needed our help to get back to the road, but he managed to get back into the wagon without too much trouble.

"Back at the stable Tom and Joe set to work on the harness to make sure it would hold together for the trip home. Roman and I wanted to clean Stanislaus up before the rest of you saw him."

"He was awful bloody," Roman assured his audience. "And the bump on his head was as big as a hen's egg – maybe a goose egg. You would have been scared he was gonna die." That comment caused some spirited conversation between the boys. Paul wished he could have seen Stanislaus like that.

Gregor continued, "Elizabeth came out of the house to see what was going on and brought water and a cloth. Then she brought Stanislaus some tea and broth and put on a clean bandage. Tom thought he should spend the night, but Stanislaus wouldn't hear of it. They gave us some dry feed sacks for a bed, and Elizabeth insisted he wear one of Tom's shirts and take the blanket. They are nice people and good friends."

Stanislaus woke up well before we got home. He was hungry and thirsty, but said his headache was almost gone. "I feel bad I caused so much trouble, he said. "In church I was remembering Easter in past years, wishing I could be back there. Then Johanna began to sing just like she always did at home, and I looked around at all the family I have here. There sat Fritz and Marianna and all their brood, and our sister Magdelana with Frank and their children, and all of you. That's when I realized we had brought "home" here to America.

"That was on my mind when I went out to get the team hitched up and I didn't notice it had clouded up and was ready to rain. The lightning strike and thunder scared me as much it did the mules, and I barely got into the wagon when they took off. That's one thing about these mules, they are as stubborn as all get out. Once they get running you have to just let them go for awhile."

It was nearly dark by the time we got home. Gregor took sleepy Stella into the house and Stanislaus helped take our things out of the wagon. I told him Gregor would look in on him tomorrow and said goodnight.

     Rita L. McWhorter

"Thank you, Johanna," he said. "And Happy Easter." Then he picked up the reins and drove off. Stanislaus was never one to linger over parting words.

The boys helped Gregor do the chores while I put Stella to bed. It had been a long day and I was grateful to be home at last.

CHAPTER 16

Spring's Glorious Plans

April 17, 1887, Sunday:
We planted the trees in the Tree Claim one warm, rainy day. Hard work, but good for the whole family to join together to get the job done.

Stanislaus has recovered from his fall from the wagon on Easter Sunday and came over to help Gregor this week. I now have a chicken coop but no fence around it, and several brooding hens from Marianna and Stanislaus. It has rained and rained in the last few weeks, and we have been aching for the sun. The ground needs to dry out before the planting can begin. Gregor plowed up the sod in my garden in the fall, so if he turns the soil again I should be able to work it well enough to get some early planting started before it gets too warm.

Yesterday was Stella's second birthday, so this afternoon Marianna and Fritz brought the children, and Stanislaus also joined us for coffee and cake. Afterwards we all went outdoors to enjoy a beautiful, sunny day. Everyone thought it was too hot for coats, of course, but some of us soon went in for warmer clothes. The north wind is still sharp and cold.

I noticed that Gregor took his planning book outside with him. Since Fritz and Stanislaus were here three years before we came, their advice is important to us and we talk to them before we make any big decisions. Marianna and I went out to follow along. Sometimes the men would rather we women didn't enter their conversations, but ever since we were building the sod house, they realize we are not here just to do the cooking. Sometimes, though, they need to be reminded that we are partners in this huge project that lies ahead.

We had a rough plan for the whole yard before we put the well down, of course, but Gregor and I labored many long winter nights over final plans and decisions. This summer the plans call for building a granary to be ready for our fall crops. It promises to be quite a nice building with a large corncrib on the left side and separate bins on the right for wheat, rye and oats. In the center will be space large enough for a team and wagon to drive through to make it easy to unload the grain. Large sliding doors will enclose both ends. We have talked to Mr. Lohmar, the builder, who says if we can get family and neighbors to help it won't cost as much. Without being asked, both men were nodding yes, of course, and pounding each other on the arm or the back and talking about what a fine granary it will be.

The talk turned next to our dream of THE BIG BARN. Gregor has spent hours with the boys telling them how grand it will be. We hope to get to work on it next year, but we need to know exactly where the barn will be before the smaller buildings are put in place. Plan book in hand, Gregor began to pace off the dimensions where he envisioned the barn would be. Fritz and Stanislaus joined him, as did we women. This led to a spirited discussion.

Stanislaus thought the plans looked just fine. Marianna wondered about water for the cows, horses, and calves that we would have in the big barn. Would we need another well closer by? Fritz questioned only one thing. Would the private lane that comes to our place from the main road curve around past the barn, and then lead to his homestead west of ours? Gregor couldn't resist teasing him a little about cutting off the only access his big brother has to the main road, but the lane was clearly marked there on the drawing.

Almost unnoticed, Roman and his cousin John had left the game Rosie had organized and joined us. They watched seriously as the men paced out the dimensions of the barn. Thirty by forty feet is huge! Roman's eyes were shining and he smiled with excitement. His boyish hand stole quietly into mine.

"Just think, Mama. Before you know it, The Big Barn will stand right there. I can almost see it, can't you?" I nodded, but when I looked around I became aware of the reality that nothing but unending prairie still pressed in close around us. The cottonwood trees we had so laboriously planted in the fall looked scrawny and frail, and the garden plot was still mostly chunks of grassy sod.

"We have a long way to go," I thought to myself. But standing there in the bright sunshine with our family grouped around us it was easier to have hope than during the long cold winter. For the first time since we left home I felt belief grow in my heart, belief that we really could make a go of a farm in the middle of this wilderness.

"Yes, Roman, now that you mention it, I think I really can almost see it." This got me a rare quick hug before he ran off to play.

Since it is still too wet to plow, Gregor plans go into town tomorrow to get the lumber to start building the granary. I reminded him that the chicken coop wasn't finished and we needed fencing wire and posts, not so much because of danger from wild animals, but so the chickens don't get lost in the wild grass. I figured that once the men got started working the fields, Paul and I would most likely be left to put in the fence as best we could, and I wanted the wire to be close at hand. If they just got the posts in for us, we might be able to handle the rest of the job.

This evening I told Gregor that I felt a little sad. "Stella is two years old, a baby no longer. And when I saw Roman show such an interest in our plans, I realized that my little boy is almost grown up, ready to do a man's job." He only nodded and quietly smoked his pipe. Then I told him that I am pregnant. He turned to me with delight in his eyes, put his pipe down and took my hands.

"How can you be sad, Johanna? This is the best news you could have told me. Looking over that Tree Claim the other day, I realized how much help it will take to farm it all. Promise me you will have a boy," he teased.

Suddenly I burst into tears. Tears are very rare for me, and at first Gregor was so shocked he didn't know what to do. It was actually a surprise even to me. Had I buried my worries so deeply that his gentle teasing brought them flowing forth? Gregor's arms went around me while he encouraged me to bring out all my hidden fears of having a baby so far away from a doctor's care.

"You know Marianna is like a sister to me," I blubbered, "and I know she is a good midwife. I was there with her when she delivered baby Karol. It's just that we are so far away from home, and my family, and our doctor, and I feel so alone, and…."

"Yes, yes, Johanna. I know, I know. You women really do have a hard life out here in this wilderness. Have you told Marianna about the baby?"

"No, I wanted to wait until I was sure. And I wanted to tell you first."

"Good for you, let me share your fears with you. You always listen to mine, and now I will listen to yours to make them lighter, just like Mama used to tell us. You don't talk about her often, but I know you miss her, especially at a time like this. Marianna will understand. She will want to know about the baby and she will be happy for you. Ask her if she thinks you should make a visit to the doctor. That might be a good idea a little later on. Promise me you will go see Marianna tomorrow." The promise was made, and my tears were finally over and wiped away.

It has been a long day, and the crying has left me exhausted. Sleep will come soon tonight. But first a prayer for a good pregnancy, an easy delivery and a healthy baby. Gregor can be the one to pray for a boy.

April 18, 1887, Monday:
My visit to Marianna this morning didn't go as I thought it would. Instead of a quiet time together over a cup of rose hip tea, I forgot about myself and pitched in to help Marianna move damp bedding outside in the sunshine and hang clothes on the line. Their house is now nearly four years old, and since the soil is quite sandy here, the sod is suffering damage from this rainy spring. Fritz and John are concentrating on the roof to stop it from leaking, and the rest will have to wait until things dry out.

As we worked together we talked about our problems with living in a sod house and how much we will appreciate living in a "real" house when that time comes. "How long will we have to wait until that happens," we wondered. Farmers don't usually put building a better house at the top of the list.

When we finally sat resting in the sunshine I told her about the baby. "I am so happy for you," she said. "I thought you had something on your mind yesterday, but with so many people around, there didn't seem to be a time for the two of us to talk. You are in good health, and I don't see any reason to expect any problems. How are you feeling?" I answered her questions and then we just talked about things all women share together when a new baby is coming.

"Even though this will be your fourth baby," Marianna said kindly, "each one is different, and your circumstances being out here will be completely different. It is important for you to prepare your mind and body for the coming months." Then she mentioned the one thing I had not thought of: I don't have any clothes for a little baby. I gave all of Stella's things away before we came to America. I should let friends and neighbors know about the baby soon so they could save their baby clothes for me.

Finally I asked her the one question I had never really talked about, I don't know why. "What do you do when you are so homesick you feel physically ill?"

She told me that first you cry, like you never cried before. Then you talk to your husband, who probably can't really understand how you feel, but will try to comfort you. He will remind you of the good things you have and whatever he can think of to get you to stop crying. "Men hate it when we cry. When you are all cried out, you go to sleep and the next day you are so busy you tuck home into the back of your mind and get on with your life. Years ago I would get very homesick, so I know what you mean, but I don't feel it so much any more. Oh, I think about my family and miss them, but I belong here now and so do you."

She was right, of course, but hearing it from her made me believe it was true.

My mind was filled with thoughts and plans for the future as I walked with Stella back home and I realized how much better I felt after talking with Marianna. A good lesson for me to remember in the future. It is only a short distance between our houses, about a quarter mile. I should take the time to do it more often.

Stella handed me a small flower she picked along the roadside. Some type of clover, I thought. It smelled so sweet and fresh. So many new things to see; so much to learn. New life was everywhere. Glorious, glorious Spring!

CHAPTER 17

Secrets of the Prairie

May 15, 1887, Sunday:

In the month since I last wrote the weather has turned warm and dry. As we planned, Gregor plowed my garden and then started on the fields. He was overtired at first because he wasn't used to all that walking and guiding the plow. Now he goes to the fields, day after day, putting in many long hours to get the job done.

The children and I have been just as busy doing chores, tending our new chicks but mostly working in the garden. It seems unbelievable how difficult it is to prepare the soil for planting. The grass has been growing here forever, so the roots run deep and are tightly entwined, even after two plowings. Sometimes I think about those huge herds of buffalo stomping around this ground as they fed here not too long ago. We still see their bleached white bones lying in bare sandy places on the prairie on our way to town. No wonder hand tools are of no use at all in preparing this grass to become a garden.

Last week Roman and I struggled with spades, sharp new ones we just bought. Paul had made no progress at all with the hoe. We were sitting in a circle on the grass, resting from our toil when I heard the meadowlark sing. I cannot express how wondrous, how exciting this song was to me. I had thought of that bird through many a dark winter's day and longed to hear his song. We looked everywhere for him but could not see him. Finally he flew right over us and perched on a nearby post. I remembered perfectly that yellow breast with the bold black V across it. It was really the first bird we'd had a good look at when we arrived here that hot day last August. Now with the sun shining on his bright spring plumage he was stunning. When he lifted his head to the sky, I quickly shushed the children. His long musical song rang out, flutelike with clear whistles and double notes, until it descended into gurgles and died away into the absolute quiet of this vast prairie. It was so beautiful it brought tears to my eyes.

Stella turned to Roman whispering, "Why is Mama crying?"

"Beautiful singing always makes her cry," he said quietly. I was touched Roman would say that. We sat there for awhile eating bread and butter, talking about what makes us cry tears of joy or sadness. We all agreed it sometimes made us feel sad to remember our home in Poland and the people we miss. "But we are getting used to being here and making this our home. I like it best when we see or hear something beautiful like the meadowlark. I always think of your Aunt Marianna and what she told me the first day we came here. She said, 'You may be surprised; the prairie has many secrets for you to discover.'" Stella wasn't interested. She just kept filling her little pail with dirt and dumping it where she was busily making her own garden.

"Look what I discovered," Paul said proudly showing us a struggling beetle in his grubby hand. "He's solid black, but see how green he is when the sun shines on his back."

     Rita L. McWhorter

Roman told us about blackbirds with red and yellow in their wings. "And one day John and I saw a flock of blackbirds near the marsh south of our place that had yellow heads." I wasn't sure if I should believe him, but I wanted to. "We plan to keep planting lots of trees to get the birds to come closer so we can see them more often."

Later on Roman took me for a walk. He thought it was too far away for Stella so we left Gregor to watch her and Paul. Actually the marsh is not all that far, less than a mile, but it was muddy and not an easy walk. The yellow-headed blackbirds were exactly where Roman said they would be, flocking together, nesting in the marsh grasses and the surrounding willow bushes. The sun had set and spread its golden glow over the scene. I could never have imagined there was such a beautiful place in the whole world. The red-winged blackbirds were there, too, the handsome male singing from his perch on a slender reed. "Kok-a-ree," Roman echoed back to the bird. It was a very special feeling to be alone with my son, just the two of us in this unusual place discovering the new things about our land. I believe Roman thought so too.

On the way back Roman casually mentioned that both his cousin John and John Dlugosh were now helping in the fields.

"Oh, I'm surprised" I admitted. "It seems like such hard work for the boys."

"John says it's easy, just a lot of walking. You get used to it, and it's really fun driving the horses."

After a pause I said, "I'm glad you told me about the two Johns. I guess that's the way it is out here, boys become men before we know it. I'll have to think about that." We walked in silence then, commenting only on the bird sounds and the big bull frog we heard.

The next day I was determined to finally get some seeds planted. I marked off a small plot I thought was reasonable and we set to work. Just when it was time for a rest we spotted Stanislaus with his mules and wagon driving down our lane. Out jumped Shep, greeting us with wild tail wagging and doggie kisses. Then we got a surprise. Stanislaus held a small bundle in his arms.

"A puppy!" cried Roman. In a moment the children were on their knees all talking at once, the puppy barking, Shep joining in and questions flying.

"Isn't he cute? Is he for us? Does he have a name? Where did you get him?" Before long I was kneeling on the ground, too, the squirming ball of black and white fur in my arms. Promises flowed. They would feed the puppy and take care of him all by themselves. Soon I was surrounded by three pleading faces and hearing the inevitable question. "Can we keep him? Please? Please?" No mother in the world could have said no.

Stanislaus answered some of the questions. "Since I was in town I went to visit the Skirving family. Tom's dog had puppies they were giving away, and I knew how much you need a dog. I liked this little guy. He was friendly, came right to me, and that tail never stopped wagging." Giving me a sidewise glance he added, "It's warm enough now so he can stay outside if you don't want him in the house." He laughed when I told him he should have been a salesman.

Then I asked his advice on dealing with the grass roots and dirt clods. He thought the best thing would be to run the harrow over it. Harrow? Then I remembered last fall asking him about the harrow that was sitting in his yard. It's a big heavy iron rectangle with fingers pointing down, sort of like a huge hand-rake in a frame. A lever to raise

 Rita L. McWhorter

and lower the frame was in high position while the harrow stood idle. Next spring he and his team would take it to a plowed field, move the lever to the down position, and pull the harrow back and forth across the field. It would break up some of the clods and make planting easier.

Stanislaus had been planning to take the harrow back to Fritz who actually owned it, but Gregor asked if he could use it since he has nearly finished the plowing. "We hadn't planned to harrow the garden since it would be hard to maneuver on such a small plot, but I could bring it over this afternoon and give it a try," he offered.

By mid-afternoon he was back with his mules pulling the harrow. Positioning the machine in the near corner of the plot, he lowered it with the lever and walking behind, guided it back and forth across the garden. The boys and I watched in wonder at how easily the harrow did the work we had labored over so long.

After a short rest Stanislaus showed us a few tricks to try. He thought it was a perfect day for our work, dry enough to use a pitch fork or hand rake to coax out the roots and throw them into a pile. He worked along with us until Gregor came back from plowing. Gregor was very impressed with how much good the harrow had done and was eager to get to work on the fields with it. The two of them were talking together when I left to do the chicken chores and make supper. Since Stanislaus had left his wagon at home when he hitched his mules to the harrow, he was faced with a walk of three or four miles. It seemed strange he left his mules with our horses and refused Roman's offer to drive him home in our wagon. "Your horses have been working all day and need to rest," was all he would say. I would ask Gregor later on what was going on. Shy as always, he declined the offer to eat with us but agreed to take home a bowl of supper for himself. (And his dog, I guessed.)

I stood admiring the garden, happily thinking that tomorrow we could plant some seeds at last. When I looked up, I saw the children still walking Stanislaus up the lane. Paul clung to one hand and Stella hung on one leg until the pace got too fast for them. Stanislaus laughed his big laugh, they returned with their thanks for the puppy and Shep cavorted with pleasure at all the action. It was nice to hear Stanislaus laugh, as we don't hear that very often. Maybe it did him good to spend most of the winter in town, where he has been working for the Skirvings, only alone in his house from Saturday nights to Mondays. I returned his final wave and moved on to my next task which was to convince three small children that the new puppy would love to sleep in the shed as he had at home, and not in bed with them.

Supper over, the room tidy, children in bed, I joined Gregor who waited in front of the house, smoking his pipe. When I asked what he and Stanislaus were talking about he explained that he had also talked to Fritz that afternoon. The three brothers had made several decisions he wanted to share with me. "The first was that Fritz would let me borrow the harrow, since Stanislaus has finished with it. The second was that we would all three share in getting the hay cut and stacked. Fritz has two mowers so I will need to buy another team of horses or mules so Roman and John can keep both mowers running, in order to cut the hay fast enough to keep ahead of the three of us doing the raking and stacking.

"The reason Stanislaus did not take his team home is that tomorrow he will take Roman to the field and show him how to use the harrow – to break him in and get him used to working like a man. I think he is ready for that," he said.

     Rita L. McWhorter

Gregor was usually sensitive about not being Roman's natural father and careful of my feelings but I could see he didn't feel the need to consult with me anymore. The decision was clear. "My" son was now "our" son (or was now "his"?) and he would work in the field. Thank goodness Roman had prepared me. I admitted it would take some time for me to get used to the idea, but we talked it over until I agreed it was the way it had to be. By then the puppy was quiet, the coyotes had begun to howl in the distance, and the mosquitoes were coming out to bite, so we went inside to bed.

~

THE PUPPY HAD SLEPT IN THE SHED BUILT LAST FALL TO store fuel for the stove, close to the house so it was easy to reach when heavy snow drifted in. Also perfect for a barking little puppy to wake the children early the next morning. As soon as the door to the shed opened the dog was everywhere, running and jumping with the three of them. After breakfast Gregor called Roman to his side with the news that Stanislaus would be over soon. They would hook Stanislaus' mules to the harrow and Roman would learn how to work the field. The puppy was forgotten as side-by-side the two men went off to work. I thought I was forgotten, too, but after a few steps Roman turned, eyes sparkling, and gave me big smile and a manly wave.

When it was time to get to work, even Stella could understand why the puppy had to stay back in the shed and out of the garden. Kneeling, my fingers in the warm earth to show Paul and Stella how to make a shallow trench for the seed bed, I couldn't help but compare this garden with the one back home. There the soil has been used for generations, hundreds of years. It is soft and easy to work. Even with our hours of preparation, this garden is far from easy. It will take years before we can expect a decent crop, I fear. But we must do what we can. My helpers worked well together and before long we had planted lettuce and other greens, peas, and carrot seeds.

Roman came back in late afternoon, hot, dirty and hungry in spite of the huge lunch I had sent with them that morning. While he had a little something to eat he told me how different it was to drive a team of mules. "They make our horses seem old and slow. I really like them." I knew he was tired but he had not a word of complaint. After he rested for a bit he started in with his usual evening chores as if it had been just an ordinary day.

Saturday was cloudy, warm and misty with gentle rain. We were sure all our seeds were sprouting already and could almost taste that first lettuce. We have not enjoyed any fresh vegetables since last fall. The carrots and turnips Stanislaus and I had put in his cellar for the winter had not lasted long, and the last few potatoes are barely edible. I still have kraut in the crock, but we were all sick of eating kraut, kraut, kraut.

So we come full circle to where I began the story of our lives in Nebraska, a complete year. There is no priest available to us just now, so Sunday is our day to rest and thank Our Lord for our good health and happiness.

Earlier today I was trying to write a letter to Mama so she could tell Mr. and Mrs. Sapok that their grandson was no longer a child, but a man working in the field. The boys were arguing again about what to name the puppy, getting louder and louder so I sent them all outside to take the puppy for a walk. Now they are back, all excited and louder than ever!

     Rita L. McWhorter

"We named the puppy! We named the puppy! Guess what we named the puppy!"

They were so noisy they woke Gregor from his nap. "Well, good," he grumbled. "And what did you name the puppy?"

"Scout!" they shouted. "He was poking his nose everywhere like a good scout looking for danger and he scared up a flock of prairie chickens so we decided he had to be named Scout."

"If we'd had a gun we could have shot the prairie chickens and cooked them for supper," Paul added. He positioned the make believe gun at his shoulder, squinted one eye, took aim and pulled the trigger. "Bang! Bang!"

CHAPTER 18

Summer's Abundance

June 26, 1887, Sunday:

The first lettuce and greens big enough to eat tasted even better than we had imagined. At first some went straight from garden to mouth, but the sand that clung to the plants soon discouraged that. The fresh peas, however, never made it to the table. Even Gregor learned he had to be at the pea patch pretty early in the morning just to get a handful. The root vegetables take a little longer, but are gradually getting big enough to eat. The small cabbage and tomato plants from the neighbors are growing well, as well as the squash and melons from the seeds we saved last summer. We planted a huge plot of potatoes, turnips and winter squash and will start eating the potatoes as soon as they get bigger than Paul's thumb. He has a favorite plant to watch. Every few days he digs down and checks out the size of the new potatoes.

Roman continues to help in the field, always willing to learn a new job. Without Roman at home Paul seemed lost for a day or two, so Gregor had a talk with him. Paul will be seven next month, and according to Papa, that is old enough to do all the things his big brother used to do. Papa was pretty much right. He has begun to see what

     Rita L. McWhorter

needs to be done in the garden without my telling him, and is sometimes digging weeds in the morning before I get there. I think it is the promise of those new potatoes that spur him on because he is not so eager to weed the rest of the garden. Remembering he fell in love with the baby chicks when they were little, I asked if he would like to be responsible for the chickens. Now he can hardly wait until we have hens so he can gather the eggs. He has helped Rosie with that chore and described to me how it feels to hold an egg in your hand, so fresh that it is still warm.

"Does this mean I don't have to weed the garden any longer?" The answer to that was, "No, and soon you will be helping with the milking, too."

June has been a beautiful month, as nearly every day there is something new to see, hear or smell. One day my back hurt so much I had to take a rest from so much bending over. Stella and I visited the marsh where the blackbirds nested and instead of going home across the meadow we made our way to the nearby road on the eastern border of our property. There is a low place on the other side of the road and a spot of bright orange caught my eye. The ground was spongy under our feet and no grass grew there. As we got closer I could see we had discovered a new flower. We admired its deep orange color emphasized by black spots on its petals. I must have seen a picture of it somewhere because I was sure it was a tiger lily. I was surprised and delighted to find this precious gem growing wild and all alone at the edge of these grassy fields. I wondered if Marianna had seen it. I could hardly wait to tell her this wonderful new secret.

Back on the road the lane to our house was but a short walk ahead. There is a small hill on the meadow leading up to this corner where the lane turns in. I had seen a riot of daisies there a few days earlier. Nearby the ground was covered with small, dainty plants that hugged the damp soil. Delicate blue flowers topped tender stems. Gently I pulled one from the soft ground. The subtle scent was so inviting I took a little bite. It was delightful, sweet and sour. Too sour for Stella. She spit it out.

On the way to Stuart last week I sat on the wagon seat with Roman who was driving. I was just enough higher than my usual seat on the floor to get a wide view of the countryside. How it has changed from the ocean of grass we first saw here last August! Many new homesteaders have moved in, all busily plowing up the fields in neat rectangles and squares. Wheat is growing tall, corn is nearing knee high, and each planted field shows a different pattern or color. Fences define property lines and keep the cows with their new calves from straying. The chimney sticking out of the roof of a new sod house seems oddly out of place but we know how important it is. New wooden buildings and structures shine in the sun. Even some roads have changed; those near town have been graded with ditches on either side for drainage.

Wild flowers, too, are fighting their way through the grass. Where cattle have grazed they have shot up and are bravely blooming. Where it is too sandy and dry for grass, flowers bloom, purple and yellow. Best of all, we have all been planting trees as fast as we can, mostly cottonwoods. Rows and clumps of them in full leaf have grown three or four feet tall.

When we got to town we checked our Post Office Box hoping for a letter from home. No letter this time, but a notice that we will have a school teacher this September.

 Rita L. McWhorter

Everyone who gets the letter should meet at the location set aside for the school house. A map is enclosed that shows the homesteads in District 205 and where the school will be built. It looks like it is straight south, a little over two miles from our house. There will be a meeting on Sunday July 3 at 3:00 PM. Frank Frost has been designated to lead the meeting to supply information and answer questions. I was talking to Franceska about it, thinking they would be in the same district, but that is not the way it is. Her John, Anna and Frank will be going to a school about a mile east of their house. The school districts were set up when the land was surveyed, and certain acres set aside for a school before we homesteaders moved in.

This is the most important development by the Government we have seen since we arrived, as far as I am concerned. Gregor and I can both read and write Polish and understand some German and Czech, but all of us need more English education. Roman's eyes really lit up when he heard we would have a school, but since Paul has never been to school, he can only ask lots of questions. There are plenty of questions for all of us beginning with where is the school house? Do we have to build it? I guess we will get the answers next week.

While we were in town Gregor bought a copy of *The Ledger*, a newspaper now being published in Stuart by Mr. W. H. Ketcham. It has a big article about the celebration to be held for Independence Day on the Fourth of July. There will be speeches and a band, riders doing tricks on their horses, games for children and all sorts of activities. We haven't been to a celebration like that in our new country, so we plan to go. Marianna says all the neighbors go and have a good time. They have food and drink for sale, but she always makes a lunch for her family to take along. "A picnic," she said. It sounds like fun and should be something interesting for me to write about next time. It has been a long time since we took a day off to attend a celebration.

CHAPTER 19

Plans for School
and the Fourth of July

July 17, 1887, Sunday:

There is an old saying about farmers: Up before the sun, labor all day but the work is never done. Now we know how true that is. Time has flown by since I last wrote almost a month ago. To be honest my bed looks better to me than my book, but so much happened already in July that I am afraid I won't remember how it went if I put it off much longer.

Looking back I now realize my last entry dated June 26th was just a week before the meeting about the school. Almost everyone in our district attended, most wearing hats to shade their faces from the hot afternoon sun. Frank was there to greet us as we got down from our wagons at the side of the road.

The grass on the school lot had been recently cut so it stood out from the taller grass of the surrounding tree-less prairie, empty and alone – until we noticed a roped off rectangle in the center where the schoolhouse would sit. We all drifted over that way as though we would be able to see the building that wasn't yet there. Some of us had brought a blanket to share and the women gathered together with their babies and young children. The men stood or squatted around the edge of the group while the older children, soon bored, went off to play. I was surprised to notice that Roman did not join them nor did his cousin John. They were men now, and stood with their fathers. Rosie was next to me and Marianna, helping with her baby brother.

Frank stood alone facing us and started by asking for two volunteers to serve with him on the School Board. Nobody really knew what he meant by "school board" but Frank had a way of clearing up all the questions quickly, usually by dodging them. Before we realized it we had voted to approve a three-man school board that would meet to hire the teacher next Sunday. Then we voted to build a sod schoolhouse (he gestured toward the roped off section) and two toilets, one for boys on the northeast corner, the other for the girls to the southeast (he pointed).

"Everyone should be here ready to help as early as possible on Monday August 1st. The men should bring spades, shovels, saws, hammers, tools, and the women should bring food and water. The School Board will see that the sod plow is here as well as the wood for the ceiling and floor, the windows and door. What doesn't get done on Monday will be finished on Tuesday. School will start September 5th and all children who will be six by the end of this year should attend."

Then he made a mistake. He asked, "Any questions?" Everyone spoke at once, waving a hand or a hat to get Frank's attention. Some began to crowd around him. Had he lost control?

He stood up tall, his arms in front of himself, hands in "stop" position. Commanding quiet in a firm voice he handled the next hour well, one question at a time. Finally it was time for the meeting to break up but Frank had one more thing to say.

"The first thing we did when all of you came here last August was to help each other build your sod houses. Today we have the opportunity to see that our children get an education. We have come together again as a community to learn how to get the job done. So come back August 1st and let's build a school!"

Frank got a good round of applause and cheers. We all left feeling friendship for each other and excited about our new school.

Next morning Gregor didn't want to hear about going to the Fourth of July celebration. "I have too much work to do," he grumped. "The weather is good and the grain is ripening. Some of it needs to be cut now before it starts to rain again."

Three very disappointed children and I looked at him in disbelief. I knew he was tired and overworked but I thought we all needed a break. Suddenly I remembered yesterday's meeting and had an inspiration.

"Lets take a vote," I suggested. "All in favor of going to the celebration, raise your hand." Gregor looked around, surprised to see our happy faces and our hands raised high.

"Women and children can't vote. Only men can vote."

"We all voted yesterday," Roman timidly offered.

"It is not an election, Gregor," I scolded keeping my voice soft. "We are in the United States of America, and I think we should learn more about Independence Day. Besides, the picnic lunch is all packed and we are ready to go."

"Are the horses ready, Roman?"

"Yes, Papa."

"Then let's go. What are we waiting for? Yes, Paul, Scout can go, too, but you will have to keep your eyes on him all day."

"Yes, Papa."

And away we went.

There was a huge crowd of people by noon and many more coming from everywhere. A stage stood right in the middle of Main Street and officials were directing the wagons to park beyond the roped off area around it. We stood on the street corner and gawked at a crowd the likes of which we had never seen before: men dressed like cowboys riding beautiful horses with fancy saddles decorated in elaborate ways; Indians wearing feathers on their heads riding sleek ponies; women in fancy clothes riding in carriages and buggies like nothing we saw around here and pulled by white horses in harness we didn't know you could buy. Musicians wandered about with their instruments in cases or in their arms. I thought I saw a whole tribe of Indians sitting around a small cooking fire, but it was only a small group of Indian women and children. Gregor had seen Indians when he went to Niobrara to register his Tree Claim, but the rest of us had never seen an Indian. Some of them were dressed like ordinary people, but some wore what we had seen in pictures, and had paint on their bodies. There were people selling various kinds of food, farmers with garden vegetables and their wives who sold baked goods. You could buy coffee, tea and jugs of beer or cider. Just the wonder of looking at all this happening in our quiet little town was worth the trip.

The announcer's voice was loud and clear as he spoke into a megaphone. He said the program would begin promptly at 2:00, and suggested we buy something to eat

     Rita L. McWhorter

and drink or take what we brought to the picnic area now. "You don't want to miss any of the fun," he yelled.

You can bet we didn't miss a thing. Saluting the flag came first, then the speeches, the serious part of the celebration. Band music and everyone singing patriotic songs was next. We all remembered the song we had learned on the train, about the spacious skies. Now we knew about the amber waves of grain, first hand.

There were races that invited the boys and girls to join, entertainers showing off their magic, their card tricks, their muscles, their shooting skills, their knife throwing, and their juggling. There were even clowns. We had such a good time we stayed until the performers were packing their gear, the Indians had gone, most of our neighbors had headed home and the announcer had put away his megaphone. Still excited, we talked about it half the way home.

Roman: Did you see that cowboy jump off and then back on his horse?

Paul: I liked that fast Indian. Especially his pony. I never thought a pony could run like that.

Stella: The clown gave me some candy and it was so good! He made me laugh.

Gregor: What did you think about the speeches, Roman?

Roman: I sure didn't understand much of the English. I'm not sure I understood the Polish, either. I would really like to learn about the Declaration of Independence and General Washington and all the presidents. I didn't even know Grover Cleveland was our president now, did you? Do you think we will learn about those things in school?

As they talked the sun set in a blaze of flame with not a cloud in sight to echo its brilliance. It was a blessing to ride along without its heat. I doled out the last of the food and water as we jostled along. Stella and Paul became bored with the conversation and took their food to the back of the wagon with the dog. Roman followed and soon all three were sprawled on the blanket with Scout in an exhausted sleep.

Gregor and I shared our bread and cheese and sipped from the water jug as we sat together on the driver's seat. I told him how impressive the speeches were to me. They were a little long, but having the English translated into German and Polish was a great idea. Listening to the speaker extolling the value of independence and freedom made me wish I had paid more attention to our history lessons in school, never dreaming that I would ever live in America. When they struck up the band and began to sing those patriotic songs, that was when my heart was stirred. When translated into Polish I understood what the songs really meant and tears streamed down my cheeks. Gregor said he knew how I felt. People all around us were wiping their eyes.

He was very taken by what the speaker said. His own pride in being Polish had suffered when we no longer had a country to call our own. He had hated with a passion being forced to join the army that had been the enemy. It made him angry to even think about it. If he had thought there was a chance of a war of independence in Poland, he said, he would have stayed and fought with them. But he didn't think there was such a chance in our lifetime.

"I am grateful to be here and glad we went to the celebration," he said. With a smile he reached over and patted my hand. We rode the rest of the way home in thoughtful silence.

 Rita L. McWhorter

CHAPTER 20

Asthma and
a Summer Storm

July 31, 1887, Sunday:

The cloudless sunset on the Fourth of July was an omen of things to come. Day after day we searched the western sky for a sign of rain as our beautiful garden wilted in the hot sun. In desperation we began a routine of early morning and late afternoon watering with buckets of water scooped from the feed tank just across the lane. It was exhausting work, but it saved most of the garden.

The garden was so important to me that I almost forgot the grain that was ripening in the fields. Rain at the wrong time could ruin the crop. Grain harvesting is another sequence like the spring cycle when the plowing and harrowing is done to prepare for planting.

The ripened grain is cut, gathered by the armload and secured into a bundle by using twine or a handful of hay or straw twisted into a rope. Several bundles are leaned against each other into a shock and left to dry out for a few days. That is when you hope for sunshine and no rain. The bundles are then transported to a threshing floor where they are flailed, causing the grain to fall to the floor. The straw is stacked outside and the grain cleaned by pouring it from one container to another while the wind blows away the chaff. The floor of our new granary worked well for this last step especially since we could open the big doors at both ends of the granary for ventilation.

The corn was in tassel and needed cultivating so cleaning the grain was left for me and the children to do. One day with a nice breeze just right we began the job, certain we could finish in a few hours. Before long I began to sneeze, then cough until I became very sick and could barely breathe. Common sense dictated that the dust was very bad for me so I brushed off my hair, washed up and went into the house. I changed my clothes, leaving the dusty ones outside to be hung on the clothesline. Roman ran to get Marianna.

Neither of us had any experience with an attack such as I was experiencing, and it was scary not to know if I would be able to catch the next breath. Gregor was even more upset than we were, so we left the children with Marianna and drove into Stuart to see the doctor. Dr. Fort had only recently come to Stuart and we are glad to have him. We used to have to go to Atkinson for a doctor, a much longer drive. The doctor asked me a lot of questions and after he examined me he said I was having an asthma attack from the dust I breathed in while cleaning the grain. There is no cure for asthma he said, and not much he can do for me. A clean, damp handkerchief or cloth over my nose and mouth might have helped but it would be best if I stayed away from such situations.

"Right now with it so dry outside if a dust storm blows up, go into the house and stay there. You must avoid heavy dust," he emphasized again. He gave me a small bottle of camphor oil saying, "I put a few drops on this cloth for you

          Rita L. McWhorter

to inhale. See if you get any relief." I nodded yes, it did seem to help a little. To both of us he said, "It also helps to calm you. If you panic you only make it worse."

Dr. Fort noticed I am pregnant and asked me a few questions. When I told him Marianna was the midwife who would deliver the baby, he said he had heard she was very reliable and trusted. She will be pleased to hear that!

～

THE RAIN INDEED HELD OFF UNTIL THE GRAIN WAS safely inside, a pretty good crop of wheat and oats considering it is our first year. Then I began again, watching every cloud, praying for rain. Finally on July 23rd after almost a month with only the smallest of showers, a violent thunder storm arrived. I remember the date because the next day was the Sunday we celebrated Paul's birthday out in the yard.

Gregor and the boys fixed up the yard to be quite comfortable. First they moved the stove outside and built a small wash-up bench near the pump. It is nice to have water close at hand when I prepare the garden vegetables. A larger table with a bench has a small roof overhead for shade. We got the idea from Fritz and Marianna. We are able to enjoy most of our meals outside now, and the house stays cooler, too.

The day of the storm was a very hot, still day. We had taken a rest after our noon dinner in front of the house. Stella and I still sat in the shade by the table, writing. We could see Gregor and the boys who had gone to the field nearby to test our new mower and our new team of horses. Roman wants to use the new team, but since he had no experience with the mower, Gregor doesn't think that is a good idea. Hopefully what they learned in the field today would help them come to a fair decision.

A faint breeze stirred Stella's paper and I realized there were dark clouds building in the western sky. Rain! I could smell it. For what seemed like an hour the clouds continued to build and I became concerned. We all know it is very dangerous to be caught in a lightning storm out in the field. Why didn't they come in? By then we could hear the thunder's distant growl and see lightning strikes in the clouds.

"Finally," I sighed when I saw Gregor and the boys unhitching the horses. Clouds, black and angry now, fought each other as they piled higher and higher. A fresh breeze sprang up. Stella and I gathered our things and went inside. We watched at the open door as the sky darkened, thunder grew louder and the lightning strikes came closer. Gregor and the boys came running toward the house. The wind now blew in heavy gusts, swirling huge amounts of loose straw, leaves and dust into the air. Just as the door closed behind them the storm began, huge drops of wind-driven rain splatted against the west window. Then came the hail, fiercely slanting in hard and fast. I had never seen hail like that before.

Would the window hold? Gregor held a heavy coat at the ready, motioning us to stand back. The wind suddenly veered and the hail began to pound straight down like buckets of icy marbles dumped from the sky. We stood across the room by the east window then, and I realized I was shaking in fear that the house would be destroyed. Huddled together we reminded each other that our house had remained steady all winter through icy gales and heavy snow storms. It would not fail us now.

The wind howled, thunder blasted again and again, loud in our ears.

"Is it a tornado?" worried Roman.

     Rita L. McWhorter

"No, the wind is not right for that. It is just a ferocious thunder storm."

It sure was. Fierce lightning cracked down again and again.

"That was close," Gregor said.

"It sure is dark in here."

"The dark is better than the lightning."

"That wind sounds brutal. The yard must be a mess."

"At least the hail has stopped."

"Thank God."

The rain continued to come down in sheets, driven by the wind. It seemed like hours, but probably less than thirty minutes later the storm moved on. Gradually the wind lost its power, the rain stopped, the thunder rumbled off into the distance. We opened the door. The sun came out shining on water streaming everywhere and small nests of hail in sheltered low spots, a rare icy treat for a child in the middle of a hot summer. The roof would need some repair but the stove sat like a rock, unshaken and unmoved. Loose boards were strewn all around. Gregor picked up a board or two, shaking his head at the work, all to be done over again. He and Roman went to check on the animals. My worry was the garden. Would it all be destroyed?

My first look left me close to tears. The wind had left its litter of straw, chaff and dirt among broken tomato vines, smashed vegetables, mangled greenery. There was hardly a sign of the neat rows of the garden we had tended so well.

Paul ran to his potato patch. "My plants are beat up, but I think they will make it."

"How about the cabbage?"

"You might have to make some early sauerkraut. But wait until I clear away some of this stuff. It's not a total loss. Look, a ripe tomato under all these vines." Paul could always see the bright side. He was right, though. The straw that the wind had blown from the dry fields had saved some of the garden. Root vegetables would probably be safe and we could replant some things for a fall crop.

The rain had come at last, but at a pretty dear price. "Be careful what you pray for," Mama used to say.

The next day we talked about the storm with Marianna and Fritz. They had gotten only a touch of hail. They would send some tomatoes over, and were sure they could help us out later if we needed anything. The men, now automatically including Roman and John, set to work rebuilding the yard furniture. Paul was proud to be seven, and a big fuss was made over the baby who had turned one year old on the 19th. Frank is a sickly child, always a worry for his parents – and for Rosie who spends a lot of time caring for him. He seems to catch every cold and germ that comes along and doesn't have a chance to get strong. A beautiful child, he felt light and fragile sitting in my lap. He gave me the sweetest smile and at that moment I knew exactly why the whole family loves him and gives him extra attention. I scolded myself for wasting my thoughts on rain. From now on I would pray for this little boy to have the strength to continue his daily battle to stay alive and get well.

~

THE GRASS IS TALL ENOUGH NOW SO THAT IT IS CALLED hay and it's ready to harvest. This will be a family project involving Stanislaus, Fritz and Gregor, with Roman and John doing all the mowing. They will stack the hay for all three homesteads and think they can finish before the end

     Rita L. McWhorter

of August. Let's hope so because the boys are all excited about going to school in September. It is all Roman can talk about.

But first comes tomorrow, Monday, August first, and we have big plans.

CHAPTER 21

Let's Build a School

August 1, 1887, Monday:

When Gregor woke me this morning it was dark and silent. "It's time to build the school," he whispered in my ear. I groaned and turned over. So he sat up and in a loud voice repeated, "It's time to build the school everybody. Rise and shine!" That got us up, rubbing the sleep from our eyes.

I started the fire to prepare a jug full of hot coffee and assembled bread, butter, plums and a poppy seed cake to take with us. Paul and Stella went to do their chores and Roman and Gregor headed for the barn. When they came back Paul said the hens were still roosting inside the chicken coop and Stella thought the rooster was grumpy. He didn't crow or eat the corn they scattered on the ground. Roman reported the cows were half asleep and not interested in being milked but somehow all the chores got done. On the way to the wagon I took a gallon jug of milk from the feed tank where it had cooled overnight and away we went. We arrived at the site for the new school at dawn to find Frank and several of our neighbors already there.

The grass had been mowed and leveled. Stakes defined the corners for the new schoolhouse. A young man I didn't recognize was driving the horses that pulled the plow, carefully turning over a long sheet of sod. I realized that the grass had been slashed into 15" x 30" blocks before it was plowed which was why he had to be so careful. Then I heard someone call the plow a "grasshopper plow." I had been answering a lot of Paul's questions as we watched, and had never heard that before, but since the insects were hopping everywhere to get out of the way we agreed it was a good name.

Wooden planks were laid on saw horses with a table cloth on top where contributions to the breakfast table were accumulating. This surprised me a little. No one had mentioned a breakfast table, but here it was happening as though it had been planned. Frank was in charge just as he had been a year ago when we had built our own sod houses. Even the weather was much the same as it had been then, sunny and soon to be hot, but this time there was a different feeling in the air. It was the older children, the ones like Roman who had loved school in their home country who generated the excitement. Roman had already convinced his cousin John, who had never been to school, that school was the best thing that could happen, and the two of them went through the growing crowd of neighbors looking for boys their age. The first question upon finding a likely possibility was, "What class will you be in?" When they found someone they would introduce him to another friend or to their brother, mother, sister or father. Most of us parents had attended school in our youth and soon caught the enthusiasm. It echoed in the talk I overheard, words like "… for the children…" "… important the children learn …" "… good the children go to school."

As we ate and chatted the sun rose higher and Frank called our attention to the work at hand. There was already a good supply of newly plowed sod and he began to direct the crew. Many put their sons to work, knowing the boys had become strong through a summer of working in the fields. Maybe they couldn't carry as much of the heavy sod as the men, but if they teamed up they could be of real help. One grassy brick at a time was put in place and the school house began to grow.

By then the women were planning the next meal. Some had brought the covered dishes with them. The rest set off in their wagons, sometimes with a neighbor and her children to go home to finish cooking the chicken or making the potato salad. As it grew warmer it became obvious more water would be needed for drinking and later for the men to wash before they ate. Another wagon set off to fetch these needs. Rosie went to pick up the food Marianna and I had prepared, so we stayed to help clear away the breakfast things and prepare for dinner. Marianna soon found the two babies she had delivered during the past year. She obviously felt a loving bond with them and their mothers. Marianna also introduced me to two other women who had talked to her about their babies and we had a nice conversation about when our babies were expected.

By noon the table was laden with platters of fried chicken, steaming mashed potatoes piled high, potato salad, slaw, huge bowls of sliced tomatoes and vegetables fresh from the gardens. Large casseroles sat on trivets or blocks of wood. Loaves of bread were being sliced and buttered down the line. Rosie and a friend stood at the dessert table to guard the pies, cakes and cookies and remind the children they had to eat dinner before they could have dessert.

There was no need to call the men to dinner. The tempting aromas filling the air said it all. Soon there were two lines of men and children at the wash stands we had

     Rita L. McWhorter

set up, eager to get to the food. We women stood ready to dish it out, worrying if there would be enough to fill up the hungry men and children. Our eyes were on an empty place on the table next to the heaps of fried chicken. Suddenly Stanislaus appeared with a big grin on his face bearing a huge ham on a cutting board that he put down on the table. An impish young girl sneaked up behind him and tied a big apron around his middle. He took it as a good joke and began cutting the ham into small slices as directed by the women around him. Some teasing from the men made him smile and laugh. He was the star of the show and enjoyed every minute. The ham was a delicious treat. Most of us had not had the time or the opportunity to butcher a hog and smoke a ham, and by now he was famous for them. He always raised a lot of pigs and said he preferred them to chickens.

We ate then while the men took a rest and the children played. Then we packed up what was left because the sun was too hot to leave it sitting too long. Some of the women took their things home along with the little ones who needed to nap out of the sun. We stayed in the shade of the wagon to watch the rest of the building and fanned ourselves with our handkerchiefs, or soaked them and laid them on the heads of the children.

Frank chose the strongest and most experienced men to finish the upper portion of the building, forming the gables, and installing the ridge pole and rafters. Enough wood to cover the roof had been supplied which was much appreciated by the builders. It would be a good, sturdy building, we could see, as they put the last of the sod on top of the roof. Wood was expensive and not all our houses had been built this well the first time.

The boys had been put to work on the teams that were building the two outhouses. They finished about the same time as the men working on the schoolhouse. Of course there was still work to be done on the inside of the school: the floor to put down, finishing touches to be made, a stove and desks to be installed. The men stood together planning when they could get away from their hayfields and harvesting to take care of all this work. Several would come on August 15, others on the 29th. Frank wrote it all down in his notebook.

It was nearly sundown by then. The kids were cranky. The women were tired. The men, young and old, were worn out. We stood around together looking with pride at the wonder we had created. It was a handsome building for sure with a sturdy door and four windows to let in enough light so the students could study their lessons. We were mighty proud.

As we shuffled around getting ready to go Frank stood on the back of his wagon and made a short speech thanking the men and boys for their work and the women and girls for their help. Then he made his final announcement:

"This is a new landmark in our lives on the prairie. This school will bring us and our children closer as we learn together. A big hand to us all!"

Cheering and clapping rang out. There was hand shaking, back slapping and some loving hugs among the women and girls as the crowd broke up. Leftover food, used dishes, pots, pans, shovels and tools were loaded on the wagons. Waving and calling goodbye to each other, the wagons headed north or south on separate ways home with one thought in mind: chores. The chickens, the cows and calves, the horses and pigs – all the animals were waiting. Evening chores still had to be done before dark, but these August days are long ones.

          Rita L. McWhorter

CHAPTER 22

Working in the Hayfield

August 2, 1887, Tuesday:
The sun was streaming through the east window when Scout's barking woke us this morning. None of us had heard a rooster crow or a cow moo.

"So much for getting an early start in the hay field," Gregor grumbled.

"Sometimes the extra sleep pays off because you can work more efficiently," I offered. No answer.

Watching how painfully slow Roman was moving I doubted his efficiency would begin for an hour or two. Our young man was not used to working as hard as he did yesterday carrying that heavy sod and I doubted any of the men in School District 205 were feeling much better.

After breakfast I asked Gregor if Frank said anything to him about the teacher. I thought it was strange Frank hadn't mentioned her. Surely he knew we all want to hear more about her.

"All he said was that he hadn't heard anything since they told him that a teacher had been hired. There are a lot of school districts in the state and it must be a big job to find so many teachers all at once."

At least he was talking now so I asked another question,

"What did you decide about the horses? Will Roman get the new team or the old ones?"

"The old ones until he gets used to the mower. Then we'll see." Gregor was almost always cheerful in the morning, talking to everyone, usually whistling, but not today. Paul, Stella and I were in the garden by the time the men got the horses ready and set off for the hayfield. We waved goodbye and Paul tried to get Scout to come back. He called and whistled, but Scout was looking for wider territory to roam. From the longing look in Paul's eyes he felt the same.

The garden had grown back far better than we had dared hope after the hail storm, especially the tomatoes. We hadn't staked them so they are spreading all over the place. They love these sunny days and are ripening fast. They taste much better than the ones we grew at home, bigger and juicier. I picked a pail full in no time and they will disappear just as fast.

I am trying to concentrate on the plants we will rely on when winter comes, carrots, parsnips, turnips, and I thought I would try beets this year. Paul knows his potato crop is vital for our winter food, for him at least. He is a potato lover who could enjoy potatoes three times a day, especially the ones he grows. I noticed that Paul had finished weeding and was at the far end of his potato patch spading up the soil. It was too early to dig potatoes, so I went to see what he was doing. He said he is digging a big hole, deep enough to preserve the root crops through even the coldest winter. His first idea was to build a cellar of sod like Uncle Stanislaus has. They talked it over and decided it would be better to start small this year with a ditch six or eight feet long. They came up with the idea to dig at the edge of the potato patch where it would be easy to dig and close to the potatoes.

"This is an experiment, Mama. Stanislaus said we can still use his cellar for the rest of our crop like we did last year. This year we use only a few potatoes. If our experiment works we can make it bigger next year." Paul's enthusiasm is inspiring. A seven year old with a passion and a goal can do a lot of digging, even on a hot summer day.

August 28 Sunday:
When I last wrote on August 2, I was reporting on Paul's cellar. Stanislaus has been busy in the hay field but I see Paul working away every now and then.

The haying has moved ahead as planned. John and Roman have the mowing routine memorized, and only need to be told when and where to mow next. This depends mainly on the weather—heavy dew or rain might determine the final decision. If the weather is fine the grass they cut in the morning dries in the afternoon and is ready to rake and stack the next day.

It has been a long summer of hard work and haying is the most tedious work Gregor has done so far, according to him. He thinks there should be machines available to make the work easier, like a rake for instance. He saw horse-drawn rakes in Europe but nothing like that here.

"Seems like if Mr. McCormick could build a reaper that can cut the grain and thresh it, too, he could invent a rake. The reaper is not perfected yet, I hear, but it's on the market. McCormick has a binder for sale, too. It doesn't do the whole job, but cuts and binds the grain. Even that would be a big help to farmers. Probably couldn't get a patent on a rake, so there would be no money in it. Trouble with machines, though, is they cost too much but I believe modern machines are the way to go. The work gets done faster so you can handle a bigger crop." I have a feeling the brothers will buy a binder next year.

After two weeks Roman was allowed to use the new team of horses as promised. About a week later Stanislaus and John came in supporting Roman between them while Gregor held the door. I didn't see any blood but Roman looked so pale and weak I was shocked. In a panic I cried, "What happened? What happened?" Scout was barking. Stella was scared and hanging onto my skirt. Stanislaus and John were trying to get Roman to sit down. Roman was trying to say something but making no sense. Everyone was trying to talk at the same time, when suddenly Fritz came in with Marianna carrying her little blue cloth emergency bag. She set it down and started to examine Roman. The room quieted down.

Stanislaus began to speak: "As far as I can figure out Roman was mowing in the lower part of the field down near the slough, you know, the marshy place where that strong, slippery grass grows, and he got a little too close to it. The mower was having a hard time cutting, causing the horses to slow down and pull harder. When they started to move up out of the marsh, suddenly the grass was easy to cut. The horses were taken by surprise and jerked forward. The mower was tilted back a little going slightly uphill and with that jerk Roman fell backwards off the seat."

John was pretty shaken but continued the story: "The horses were pulling the mower without Roman on it, heading toward where Uncle Stanislaus was working. So I stopped and raised the mower bar so I could get to Roman fast and yelled to Uncle for him to catch the team. When I first got to Roman I thought he was dead but then he started to breathe and I knew the wind was just knocked out of him.

 Rita L. McWhorter

"Lie quiet, lie quiet," I kept saying but he wanted to sit up so I knelt down behind him and let him lean back on my legs. That was when I felt the lump on the back of his head. When Papa and Uncle Gregor drove up in the wagon they got a wet rag for his head. He could hardly walk but we got him loaded into the wagon and brought him home."

Marianna said something to John, nodding her head, I guess telling him he did the right thing, and turned to Gregor who wanted to know if we should take him in to see the doctor.

"Seems to me ten miles in the wagon over these rough roads is not what Roman needs just now." She had been gently feeling his lump and looking him over for broken bones or other injuries. Turning to me she said, "I can't find anything seriously wrong with him. That's a pretty good bump on his head, though. Keep a close eye on him for an hour or two and call me if he doesn't look right. Let him eat and drink if he feels like it, and go to sleep at his normal time. The wet rag was a good idea, John. That will help the swelling go down. Give him a day or two off the job, Gregor." She got a clean cloth out of her bag and directed John to wet it out at the pump. When he came back she replaced the first rag with a colder one.

My prayers were heartfelt that night. Over and over I thanked God for watching over us. After a day at home Roman was begging to go back to mowing. It was such a scare for me I had a terrible headache for the next three days, but I had to let him go back to work.

The rest of the month passed without any more trouble. Now there are four good-sized stacks of hay in the pasture near the corral with a fence around them to keep the cows away. When the heavy snow piles up this winter it will be a comfort knowing that feed for the animals is close by. This business of having animals to care for during the winter takes a lot of planning and Gregor is building up quite a herd of cattle to care for. It doesn't seem to bother him, though. Now he's talking about getting hogs next spring. And the corn hasn't even been harvested yet.

When I write about Marianna I realize how much we depend on her. Most of her medicine knowledge came from her mother, especially cleanliness. Her mother believed it was just common sense that dirt and grime are not good for a wound or a sick person. Marianna listens to anyone who can teach her about medicine. If someone is going to visit the doctor, she offers to go with them so she can listen and ask questions. The last time she saw Dr. Fort in Stuart he said he depended on her to take care of this part of the country because it was so hard for him to get out here. He told her she would have made a good doctor. She is very proud of that and so am I. We are lucky to have her only a quarter of a mile away.

I haven't met the teacher yet but her name is Agnes Braun. She comes from Atkinson and will board with the Krysl family who live only about a half mile from the school. She has her teaching certificate, understands Polish, Czech and German and speaks good English. Frank says she is a young girl but she looks plenty strong and capable of handling the bigger boys just fine. I can't wait to hear all about her when Paul and Roman get home from their first day of school only one week from tomorrow. Oh, where did the summer go?

     Rita L. McWhorter

CHAPTER 23

School For The Children

September 5, 1887, Monday:

Usually I write on Sunday but today is the first day of school and I wanted to record this important, exciting day. All of us awakened early, as always, as chores were finished by sunrise when all the signs predicted a hot day. That meant water to carry for all the animals to drink, an extra chore for the boys to help with. Roman grumbled a bit, saying there always seemed to be an extra chore of some kind before breakfast. He was right; the work is never done.

Gregor was in a hurry to get out to the field before the sun got too hot so I packed his dinner pail and a mug of coffee to take along with his jug of water. He looked rather lonely sitting in the wagon with no helper but then I noticed he had Scout tied inside the wagon for company. No dogs allowed at school.

It takes more than an hour to walk the two miles to school, but well before it was time to go the boys had washed up, changed their clothes, put on their shoes (they had been barefoot all summer) and slicked down their hair. Roman picked up their dinner pail and went out just as their cousin Rosie came down the lane by herself.

"Isn't John coming?" Roman wanted to know.

"No, he has to help Papa in the field. He wasn't very happy about it but Papa said he will be able to go to school later on. Maybe next week."

"How about the twins?" I asked.

"Mama decided it was too far for them to walk on such a hot day. So this time it's just me."

"Well then, let's go!"

Off they went at a good pace, Paul barely keeping up. Rosie reached for his hand but he was having none of that baby stuff and pulled away.

"Roman, slow down!" I called out. "Remember what I said about not leaving your brother behind? You are responsible for him until you get inside the school house."

"Yes, Mama, don't worry, we'll watch out for Paul." All three set off running. Before they were out of sight they turned to wave goodbye to Stella and me.

I hadn't thought about how we would feel when they were gone. It seemed like everyone was off to an exciting adventure and we had been abandoned. Big tears filled Stella's eyes and she buried her face in my apron. I didn't know how to explain my own mixed emotions even to myself. I was glad the children had a school to go to, proud of my handsome sons who set off so bravely, but they were growing up so fast. And yes, I was feeling all alone. My eyes were moist as I picked Stella up and held her close. "Come, we will find something special to do, just the two of us." Soon the kitten realized the dog was gone and she rubbed against our legs to get our attention. We weren't alone after all.

The boys came dragging home well before I expected; their school day was supposed to end at 4:00. The pump was their first stop. They took turns pumping, splashing

     Rita L. McWhorter

water on their faces to cool down and getting a long drink of water. Then we sat in the shade for a bite to eat and to hear about their day.

Roman began, "We got there early so we got to meet the teacher, Miss Braun. She was standing at the door to meet everyone as they came in. When the others began coming she told us to go ahead into the hallway. The last time we saw it was when it was empty. Now when you first go inside there is a small bench on the right side with a pail of water with a dipper and a pan beside it for washing hands. The door to the classroom is next to the bench. Across the hall are coat hangers in a plank on the wall and in the northwest corner is a big bin filled with kindling and wood for the stove."

"Today the door between the two rooms was open and the first thing I saw was the stove. It is standing in the middle of the room like a queen, new and shiny with a chimney that goes straight up through the roof. It is surrounded by rows of long narrow tables with benches attached to them in all sizes, the biggest ones near the back of the room. The teacher's desk and chair are in the front of the room facing us. There is a blackboard across most of the wall behind her desk. The ceiling and floor are wood and the walls are painted white. It is really nice. You should come to see it, Mama. And the biggest surprise? In the southeast corner is an American flag on a pole and on the wall is a picture of George Washington, 'the Father of our Country,' the teacher told us."

"Miss Braun has a bell on her desk. She rang it really loud, and everyone shut up. She said thank you in Polish, Czech and German and introduced herself. In English she said, 'In school we will speak English.' In all three languages she said to raise our hand if we could tell her what she just said in English. A few hands went up, mostly girls, but I didn't know for sure if I had the right answer so I didn't raise mine."

"She motioned for us to stand up and announced, 'Now we will divide into classes by how old you are.' Starting with age five, first in English then translated, she went up the ages until everyone was seated. The last one was a girl 16 years old – all the big boys were really looking at her."

"I bet they were. That must have taken a long time, didn't it?"

"Not really. There were only 9 of us there. I thought we would have a lot more, but I guess it is a busy time and most of the children are helping in the fields or herding the cows or watching the little ones while their Mama helps outside. It moved very fast and if anybody talked or got noisy she rang the bell and held her finger to her lips. Everybody did what they were told or she looked at them with a really mean face. Most of the time she smiled."

"There was still time for her to show what we would do every morning before we started classes; it's called Opening Exercises. First we stood, put our hand over our heart and faced the flag while she said the words in English that she explained were the salute to the flag. Then she sang — in English, a song about America. It was beautiful. When it was over the room was completely silent. Then one of the bigger girls started to clap and we all clapped."

"Someday I will know that song well enough to teach it to you and Papa – and yes, you too, Stella."

"Does she have a nice voice?"

"Oh, yes. You can tell she loves to sing. Like you, Mama."

"Paul, what were you doing all this time?"

"I was quiet. I didn't want her to give me that mean look."

     Rita L. McWhorter

I had to smile at that.

Roman continued: "Recess came next. We went outside to go to the toilet and play for a while. Paul went by himself. When it was time to go inside Miss Braun rang the big bell that is on a post by the door."

"After that she sat behind her desk with a big book and called each of us up to the front according to our age. The youngest was a little boy who was six. His big sister had to go with him up to the desk because he was scared to go alone. Miss Braun asked some questions in whatever language was necessary and wrote down the answers. That was interesting because we learned everyone's name and what grade they would be in. Miss Braun told us where to sit. There were plenty of empty places but I guess they will fill up when we get more children coming to school."

"It was noon by then. Miss Braun brought her dinner outside to eat with us in the shade on the north side of the schoolhouse. We talked about games we could play and she suggested we ask our parents to remember some of the games they played when they were our age."

"There is always tag," I offered.

"That's what I said, and we did play tag, but it was really hot in the sun. We didn't stay out very long. It felt cool when we went back inside. We put our heads down on top of our arms on the desk and listened to a story. It was hard to understand because Miss Braun mixed up all the languages we speak with English. She said that way we would all learn to understand each other as well as those in our new country. Miss Braun handed out English books to most of us and gave the younger ones some small things to keep them busy."

"It was very quiet. We had opened some of the windows on the north side but there was no fresh air coming in.

There were no birds singing. Nothing moving. We looked at our English books. I could see that some for the younger ones had pictures. Mine had no pictures. I felt like it would be impossible to ever make any sense out of it and closed it."

"At last Miss Braun said, 'Since it is our first day and it is so hot I have decided to dismiss school early.' She said to please put our books on the shelf under our desks. Make a line according to how we sat, little ones first. 'Take your time. No pushing. No talking. I will sing us out with a song in English. Don't worry, you will learn it sooner than you think.' I learned a little of it."

"She sang until we all got out and we all started talking at once and going back in the hall to get our dinner pails and other stuff."

"Did you say thank you?"

"Oh yes, everyone thanked her. She is very nice."

"Is she pretty?"

Paul answered without pause, "When she smiles she is pretty, but not when she gives that mean face."

Later on as we did the evening chores I overheard Roman telling Gregor the same story, and heard him laugh. It must have been the part of the story when Paul answered the question, "Is she pretty?" I will have to meet Miss Braun soon to see if she can teach me the mean look that makes boys behave.

Last night just as sleep overcame me the sound of Miss Braun singing was in my ears. Imagine that, a school way out here in the middle of the prairie with a young teacher who likes to sing. When we get our choir, I will have to ask her to join. What a blessing!

     Rita L. McWhorter

CHAPTER 24

A Short Autumn

September 25, 1887, Sunday:

We had sunny days early this month so I was able to dry some late tomatoes and whatever fruit and berries I could get my hands on. It feels more like fall now and I am thinking about all the work we need to do next month before the baby is born in November. I went with Stanislaus one day last week to help get his cellar ready for the food we need to store there. As we swept the shelves we were remembering last year when we had been in America only a month or so. We had no time to grow a garden of course, and depended on him and Fritz and Marianna for supplies for the coming winter. I told him that looking back I realize how little we understood about winter out here on the prairie. I told him again how much we appreciate his help.

"I am determined to have a lot more food stored this year," I explained. "There were times last year when our supplies got very low. Too often we were so heavily snowed in we couldn't get into town and it worried me. What would we do if we had nothing at all to feed the children? That is not a good feeling."

Then we got on the subject of sauerkraut. Stanislaus said he wouldn't be making kraut this year because it didn't agree with him anymore. If I wanted to use his crock to make more for us, I was welcome to it. He planned to see if he could trade some of his cabbage for apples and other fruit that was coming in by train lately. That sounded good to me and I mentioned that if he thought I could trade anything from my garden for fruit to let me know. Stanislaus spends a good deal of time in Stuart, mostly helping out in the lumber yard. He is planning to spend most of the coming winter in town. He says it is too cold and lonely for him out here.

When we got home the boys were waiting for us. We all went out to the garden to see if any of the potatoes or carrots were going to be ready for storage soon. They reported everything looked great and would be a very fine crop very soon. Stanislaus advised that we check again in two weeks, and start digging the potatoes as soon as they were a decent size.

"I remember last year the snow came so early I had to leave some of my crop in the ground to rot," he said.

October 9, 1887, Sunday:
Two weeks later I knew Paul had listened to his uncle's advice. I found him in his potato patch taking samples here and there. Some of the potatoes were a really good size and he wanted to know if he should dig them up. It seemed a little early but the weather had turned cold lately and I supposed it could snow any time. I recommended he go ahead and dig up the big ones. He could ask Stella to help gather them into a pile near the edge of the garden. I promised I would look over the garden and see what else was ready to harvest. We would get our first wagon load of food and other provisions safely into the cellar before it snowed.

     Rita L. McWhorter

Today Marianna and the family are visiting and we got to talking about how miserable it was last winter. We remembered how terribly cold it was for weeks on end, how the snow piled up so high everywhere we could barely move around on foot. Just keeping our animals alive was a struggle, and we ended up butchering a lot of them before they died. We stored the frozen meat mostly in the shed next to the house. There it was safe from the wild animals who were starving and we could get to it easily. Fritz reminded us of the many herds of cattle that were lost throughout the area during the worst of it. Driving a team of horses pulling a wagon was often impossible. Even the trains couldn't run when the tracks were completely covered with tons of snow from one blizzard after another.

Suddenly Marianna stood up and began to put on her coat.

"That's enough now about last winter," she announced. "We have to forget about the past and face what we have to do now." We had only a few minutes to thank Marianna for her good sense before they were out the door and waving good-bye as they trooped down the lane.

Gregor and I sat down then and made a list of things we had to do immediately. Roman understood when he was told he would have to put going to school aside and work with Stanislaus in the cornfield. Paul would be the man at the spade, ready to dig up whatever was needed. I tried to think of all the individual garden food that needed to be put into the cellar. Finally I realized that would be a separate list for me to make. For the big list they would be one item called garden food. We also had to make sure the grain had been made into flour and the oats into meal. Did we have enough fuel to keep the stove burning? That was only one of the many questions we had to ask ourselves as the list got longer and longer.

Johanna's garden food list: Potatoes, carrots, parsnips, green tomatoes, squash, cabbage, onions, garlic, apples, dill, parsley. These would all have to be loaded into the wagon and stored in the cellar with clean dry dirt to spread over the root plants.

Gregor added: Gather wood, chips, sticks, willow branches, slippery grass from slough. Move more haystacks near the house. Take wheat, oats and corn to mill. Make a special trip to town to buy extra sugar, salt, dried fruit and any usual supplies that are running low.

Before we had supper that evening Gregor held up the list we had made.

"This is what we must get done before winter sets in. We will have to work hard to take care of all these jobs but I'm glad we have a list. We will check them off, one job at a time, and make sure we do some of it every day."

Later that evening as we talked about the list, he confessed to me, "I have a feeling that more than likely we will add to the list as we go along, and not cross many things off. We will always have more to do." I had to agree.

          Rita L. McWhorter

CHAPTER 25

Winter of 1887

October 30, 1887, Sunday:

The last time I wrote (on October 9), we had made a serious list of tasks that we would have to complete but we had not set a goal to meet except "before winter sets in." The very next morning we learned winter might be here sooner than we thought. Everything was covered with the first frost of the autumn season and suddenly we knew it was time to harvest everything that might be killed by the next frost. We left the chickens alone although we knew we'd run out of feed for them, because if last winter was any indication, we'd lose some to freezing and could then butcher as the winter passed. They didn't lay much in the winter, but any eggs we could get would be welcomed. We hoped to winter over the cows and horses, of course, and have calves in the spring, if we could. Some things in farming are always left to chance, after one made their best bets. This much we had learned the hard way.

We all got to work and the first time Stanislaus brought his wagon that was not filled with corn, we loaded it up with our collection of squashes, tubers and roots and our bushel baskets of green tomatoes. Smaller lots like strings of dried fruits and summer squashes would hang from our rafters at home. He drove us over to his place and helped us get all of the garden food safely stored away. We'd check it frequently and eat the things first that wouldn't last, and as winter passed we'd adjust our menus to fit what needed to be used up. Filling the cellar didn't mean the whole list had been checked off, but we had made great progress and I was feeling relieved. Now I could concentrate on having my baby.

Marianna did come over shortly after that and scolded me for working so hard, but I didn't take her too seriously. She knows only too well that out here there is no alternative but to do what needs to be done. She checked my baby's position and asked me questions, and said everything seemed to be normal and the baby should be ready to come in a week or two. She said to send the children over as soon as I felt any pains, especially if there was any chance of a big snowfall. She warned me not to be left alone even for just a little while, and to rest so I'd be strong for the delivery.

On Tuesday November 8 we had a big snow storm with enough wind to pile it up. I thought for sure the baby would choose to come then, but nothing happened. By Saturday things felt well in hand. We had paths to all the important places, including to Marianna's house, not good enough to drive a wagon on some of them, but at least good enough to walk safely. I started to have pains that morning, and around noon I alerted Gregor to be ready to go for Marianna. As we were talking about it, Fritz came to the door to see if he was yet needed. He suggested the children bundle up and go back to their house with him. Each one carried a pillow and a blanket, ready to spend the night. Roman brought Marianna back a little later. He and Gregor finished up the evening chores, left a lantern for us "just in case" and with our promises that everything would be fine, they said

     Rita L. McWhorter

goodnight and closed the door. My men were good ones. I could hear them laugh and whistle a tune as they drove away in the gathering dark.

It was strangely quiet for a little while, but we talked about what we could probably expect next, had a small meal and tried to get a little sleep. Shortly after midnight my water broke and everything proceeded in an ordinary way. We had set aside plenty of extra sheets and cloths, had water on the back of the stove, and the woodbox was full. It was long, hard labor but with no problems. The baby was born well before dawn, a strong little boy, just what Gregor had told me he wanted.

Marianna and I had become very close these last few months. The night baby Stencil came into the world, we were bonded by the birth. We worked together in a silent house made of the sod, a small place in what seems like an endless prairie. The only sound was our voices until the baby came with a lusty cry of triumph. We joined him with prayers of thankfulness and relief. I watched Marianna write it in her book: "Born Nov 13, 1887, baby boy, name: Stencil (Stanislaus) Hytrek."

We got little Stencil cleaned up and things quickly into good order. Marianna was all smiles and congratulations, happy that everything had gone so well. I had to have a little cry before I could enjoy the wonderful outcome. I had worried so much about all the dire possibilities and now I felt only a great lifting of that worry, my heart full of gratitude.

Gregor came in soon after, brushing fresh snow from his clothes and stamping his feet. Marianna assured him everything was fine while he took off his coat. He couldn't wait to hold the little bundle and welcome his new son. We drank hot tea and shared bread and butter together, but it was easy for Gregor to notice the three of us were very tired and needed a few hours rest. He said he would finish the chores and come back home later in the afternoon. He left us sleeping as he quietly went out the door to spread the good news to the chickens and cows, and then to our neighbors.

As promised he came back with our family and Fritz came with theirs. The children were very impressed with how tiny this baby was, and checked to make sure he had the proper number of fingers and toes. Our helpers didn't stay long because it was still snowing, but they left us a big pot full of soup for our supper. It was a very thoughtful and delicious gesture. We would be lost without them.

The baby and I spent a few days learning how to nurse and then were both well on our way to getting strong and healthy. The snow stopped falling for a while but it remained wickedly cold most of the time. Even the sun had little effect trying to melt the big snow banks that were everywhere. The men talked about the January thaw that frequently came. It was something to bring hope, but none of us felt we could count on it for sure. Winter was always longer than anyone wanted it to be, and we were not even in the middle of it yet.

We knew Christmas would come, however, no matter what. I had realized that it would most likely be hard to do much about the holiday, so months before I'd secretly prepared. Small presents were safely hidden away and sugar, flour, poppy seed and other important ingredients were waiting to be made into some of the things we loved to eat at holiday time. Stella helped me bake a few of the simpler foods and I tried to show her the secrets I had learned as a child. The smells made me nostalgic for the history and tradition of the old country, but I comforted myself with the knowledge that back there, it was all still in place. Just

     Rita L. McWhorter

we had changed our location, though not our heritage. The kolaches tasted almost as good here in America, with the clean butter from our sturdy cows.

Everything was solidly frozen on Christmas Eve but Gregor and Roman went out to check the animals midway through the long evening, having done the chores early to dress up and celebrate. When they returned they reported they could hear ringing bells. All of us put on our coats and went out to listen. The sky was filled with stars and the night was completely silent except for the creaking of our footsteps in the hard snow. Softly the bells rang from far, far away. We wanted to stay to listen, but it was so cold we had to go inside after only a few minutes. We talked about the bells, all of us excited, wondering if the sound came from town or if they were a Christmas miracle straight from heaven. It brightened our conversation and led to stories of the birth of Jesus. We sang all the carols we could remember. Roman sang one in English he had learned at school. Finally we pushed our mattresses close together as near to the stove as we dared and Gregor quietly sang his favorite carol as we all went to sleep. It was one Christmas we would surely never forget.

CHAPTER 26

Our Coldest January

January 1, 1888, Sunday:
Today Stanislaus came home. He had been living in town
since the weather turned cold. By Christmas there was so
much snow no one could travel anywhere, even to church,
unless they lived quite close to their destinations. He likes it
where he lives in Stuart but I think he got very homesick for
the open spaces and the children. The newspaper in Stuart
had heard our news and Stencil's birth was reported in a
small article, which made him even more ready for a visit.
He also guessed that with a new baby, we might have found
it hard to get over to his cellar for the food we had stored
there. He was always so good about thinking of others, a
trait we hoped would be passed to his namesake.

Finally he and his friend Henry decided to give traveling a try. They agreed to start out early and if they hadn't
made it more than halfway here by noon, they would turn
around and go back to town. They hooked Henry's team
of horses along with Stanislaus' mules to the wagon and
were surprised at how well the four worked together. He
told us about how hard it was finding a way through and
around the snow banks that they ran into, but they knew
the landscape well and could sometimes read the snow to

know if it was packed or in softer drifts. The occasional fences kept them oriented and each farm they passed helped them know they were on the right track. No one was outside the houses, but they could see the smoke from their stoves, and noted that most people had ropes from their houses to their privies and barns, or rows of stakes, as well as well-worn paths to follow. The soddies sat low in the drifts and looked cozy and warm, with ample haystacks nearby and piles of firewood covered with little stick roofs as people had always done. No one else was traveling, so they felt like great adventurers.

They made it to his house by late afternoon without getting seriously stuck, and that is where they spent the night. They were bone-tired from the constant cold and very grateful Stanislaus had left food and fuel in the cellar before he left. The stacks of hay near the house were a welcome sight for the animals as well, and Stencil reported that his dog, a useful foot warmer, had settled on the bed as if they'd never been gone.

It was such a surprise to see them at the door the next day. Their arms were full of food and supplies we hadn't seen in a long time. "And more in the wagon," Stanislaus said. The best part of the surprise was Stanislaus when he saw the baby. He knew we were naming the baby after him, so seeing the new one was what he really had been looking forward to. Immediately he had his hat and coats off and this tiny baby snuggled in his arms. At first he bounced and talked softly to Stencil while he tried to tease a little smile out of him. When he finally got a response he broke into laughter so loud the baby began to cry, his signal to quickly give him back to me. To hide his emotions he stuck his head out the door to check on Shep and Scout, who were running and playing like wolves in their thick winter fur.

We spent a few hours listening to the news from town, the dogs allowed in to stretch out under the stove as we all gathered around it. The most interesting thing to me was that the newspaper was now receiving weather reports from the government, by telegraph. His friend Henry sometimes reads interesting articles to him, so they knew the temperature had been well below zero in most of the states around us. One day there was no report of the temperature at all. It seems it was so cold their thermometers were frozen. At first he thought that was kind of funny. You didn't really need a thermometer. All you had to do was go outside and you knew it was colder than any weather we had ever had before. Then Henry told him about the new department the government was developing to study the weather. They were inventing new instruments and hoping to be able to soon issue timely warnings of threatening storms to people everywhere in the country, just as they did for ships along the coasts, with flags and symbols. The warning flag for extreme cold would be white with a black square. That started an interesting discussion for me to listen to while I cooked a hot meal for us to eat together. It didn't seem that hanging a white flag, in a blizzard, at a train station, would be much help to people on the plains like us, but we supposed that one thing the government did like to do was to keep track of things, so there would be no end of instruments and measurements, whether they were helpful or not. We didn't need the numbers to know enough to stay inside where it was warm.

Soon after eating Stanislaus and Henry got ready to leave, saying they had to get to town by tomorrow before

     Rita L. McWhorter

another bad storm came. Promising to come back soon they went off with our thanks and our wishes for them to have a safe trip over the vast expanse of snow between us and the town. Perhaps they could retrace their route and it would be a little easier on the horses, and perhaps the winds would be light and at their backs. As we watched them disappear in the white, we knew they'd have to be not only smart, but lucky. But of course, we all thought spring would come, and we'd be there to sing about it.

January 8, 1988, Sunday:

Today, only a week later, and Gregor is stamping the snow off his boots not long after he had gone out to do the chores.

"I know exactly what Stanislaus was talking about when he told us we would recognize when the temperature is well below zero. In only minutes you can barely breathe, your throat begins to feel raw, your lips are dry, tears sting the corners of your eyes and you know you don't dare stay out any longer than the short time you have been out. I'm worried about the animals. Where would we be without our cows and horses? Even though they are sheltered and fed they are stamping to keep from freezing. They need water, too. We will have to try to melt more snow.

"No one goes out that door today without my permission! Understood?"

Such a stern father was seldom heard in our house and we all took him seriously. It is dangerous to go out.

January 12, 1888, Thursday:

I am writing the date here because I want to mark this beautiful day. Gregor had gone out before dawn to see to the animals and stayed out longer than usual. "I can hardly believe it." he said when he came in. "Compared to these last few weeks it is really warm out there."

Roman was next to get up and open the door. "I don't see any clouds and the sun will be rising soon." Before long the sun was casting golden rays on the icy snowbanks and if you stayed very quiet you could feel a tiny warm breeze from the southwest every now and then. It was the most beautiful morning we ever had.

"This must be the start of the January thaw I hear Uncle Fritz talking about. We might have a whole week of nice weather and all the snow will melt," Roman said. Just then we could see Fritz and John coming slowly up the lane.

"It's not easy going yet," Fritz grumbled. "The ice on top of the snow banks is melting making it even harder to get through some places than it was an hour ago. I came to see if you were all enjoying this fine morning."

We all began talking at once about how wonderful it was to have such a lovely change. "You are the old timer here, Fritz," Gregor said. "What do you think about this? Too good to be true?"

"I have to admit I have never seen weather like this, neither the terrible cold nor this sudden change. I think we should enjoy what we have today, but don't count on it to last. Get your important work done as fast as you can. Keep your eyes open, watch the sky, the clouds, the sun, and don't get too far from home." That sounded like wise advice, but I thought Fritz seemed more worried than glad to have the break in the weather.

"We have to get back to our place now and follow my advice. Good luck to you."

We went inside to eat and make our plan for the day. Before Gregor could tell me what I should do I wanted him

          Rita L. McWhorter

to know what I thought was most important. The shed next to our house had gotten completely out of order. "We can't find what we need and don't even know what is in there anymore. Stella can be my helper and can keep her eye on the baby at the same time."

Gregor wanted to get a load of hay if possible and would need Paul's help.

"Roman, you will have the hardest job. First I want you to take back the knife we borrowed from Uncle Stanislaus. From there the Frost place is only about a half mile. Your Uncle Frank has some spices for me. If the meat I have frozen thaws out I will have to make it into baloney. It wouldn't taste very good without those spices. But you heard what Uncle Fritz said, 'Get your important work done as fast as you can.' You will have to explain that you can't stay to visit but turn around and come straight back home."

Roman was delighted. He hadn't been able to see his cousins for a long time and even a quick visit was exciting. He went off with a wave and a whistle, and Scout for company.

~

A FEW HOURS LATER A BIG BLACK CLOUD COVERED THE sun and darkened the sky and a roaring, freezing wind is blowing heavy snow like we have never seen before. We are terrified because Roman has not come home. Gregor has made several attempts to look for him but the wind is so strong it takes away his breath and knocks him down. The snow is filled with small, sharp bits of ice or sand that hurts when it strikes you. You can see nothing, he says. It would have carried Gregor away if he hadn't dropped to the ground and crawled back into the house. We are praying

Roman stayed at his Uncle's house or has found shelter with a neighbor, but there is no way to find out until the storm dies down. We are helpless with nothing we can do but pray. I am so worried that I can't get out of my head that Roman is out there lost and calling for me. Gregor tries to get me to sleep but I can't stop crying.

Rita L. McWhorter

CHAPTER 27

The Blizzard of 1888

January 13, 1888, Friday:
It is early, still dark, quiet. A noise! What is it?

Gregor threw off his blankets and flew to the door. Frozen, hard to open. Fritz and Marianne stumble in along with an icy blast of outdoor wind. Behind them, outside, John Prince ties his horse to a post, comes in and shuts the door. Gregor, shaking his head, tears in his eyes, saying over and over, "No, Roman did not come home. Roman is lost. He did not come home."

Fritz tries to comfort him. Marianna comes to me.

John joins our tearful greetings. "I saw Roman just as the storm hit, but he couldn't hear my calls. The wind tore my voice away. The snow blinded me, I couldn't breathe and I knew I was lost. I put the reins down and let my horse take me home. But I was afraid for Roman."

Frank pushed the door open. The sun was on the horizon spreading color but no warmth.

"I worried all night about Roman, I thought I saw him just as the storm came. Now we have to move quickly to find him."

(I am writing this the day after the worst blizzard anyone here has ever seen or heard about. Marianna just went home but not until she made me promise I would sit down and write in my book about this terrible time. She said it might help me stop crying if I had something to do besides worry about Roman. She is concerned I might lose my milk if I don't do anything but cry.)

It was just like Frank to have a plan. "We can't meet here, Johanna has enough to take care of without a house full of men coming and going. We can all go to the schoolhouse and use it as our meeting place. We will put together all the information each one of us has about Roman's movements, about the storm and especially the wind direction. Using all that we know we can organize as many search parties as we can get volunteers. Since the temperature is still below zero and the snow and ice will slow us down, we will have to be careful no one stays out too long. Frost bite might be our worst enemy and we can't afford to put anyone on the sick list."

Later that day Henry Krobot brought Scout home to us. The dog had gone to the Krobot place yesterday while the storm still raged. He was in bad shape, coat frozen with layers of snow and his paws bleeding. He said they knew it was Roman's dog but couldn't imagine why he would be so far from home. Henry gave him warm broth and gradually thawed him out last night. Stella and Paul were overjoyed to have him home and thanked Henry again and again. I told Henry that Roman had not come home and the men were at the school organizing search parties. Henry didn't hesitate. He said he would go to the school now. He gave the dog a hug and warned us to keep Scout's feet bandaged until they got better. Without another word he gave us a wave and went back out in the cold.

I now have hope that knowing where Scout went for shelter will be the information that the searchers need to

     Rita L. McWhorter

find Roman. I think it indicates the wind pushed him much further south than we could have guessed.

Meanwhile it is time to get Paul and Stella to help me prepare the vegetables for a big pot of stew. For hours they have been faithfully twisting hay into small bundles to burn in our stove. Having Scout home is a blessing even though he is suffering from fatigue and his sores. I expect it will take several days for him to heal. I feel a little more hopeful that knowing where Scout was will give the search parties information to help find Roman.

CHAPTER 28

Welcome Changes

February 12, 1888:

It is a month since we experienced the blizzard that took away our Roman and so many others as they struggled with all their might to get home. Gregor tries to shield me from so much bad news but somehow it leaks in to us. Meanwhile, the cold weather has not budged a degree. Groups of search parties continue to go again and again over the snow and ice that cover the prairie looking for Roman. There is no sign of him anywhere.

The day after the storm all the men who braved the hard weather knew they would have to work quickly to find Roman still alive. They went out in groups, hopeful they would be successful. When they learned that Scout had turned up in an area they hadn't covered, they decided to search the area further south the next day. By the end of the second day they realized Roman would have been out in the cold for three days and nights. Failure to find him was hard to take.

When Gregor came home that evening he had no strength left and I knew he had lost hope that Roman could still be alive. I was stunned. Not once had I thought about giving up hope, and I didn't know how to do it. For me, if there was no hope there was nothing. All I could do was cry. Before many days passed I had no milk to feed my baby, and he joined me with my crying.

It's just as well I have no real memory of the following days. I know Marianna was often with me and there were others with kind voices and gentle hands helping me. Later I learned that many family members and neighbors had come to help feed the baby and take care of the family. One afternoon when Stencil finally went to sleep it was Gregor who came to me. He put his strong arms around me and talked in a soothing voice. He said he finally realized what I meant when I said I didn't know how to give up hope. He understood that I had never been faced with such a terrifying challenge before. To explain what he meant, he went back to his past when he fought in the war.

"Death was everywhere," he said. "In order to survive I had to learn how to accept the finality of dying. It has nothing to do with crying or pushing your thoughts away. You have to make up your mind that you must do it by yourself. You must ask God to help you, yes. But you have to believe you can find the strength to face the truth. We know that Roman's body is frozen in the snow nearby but his soul is in Heaven. He is with God without the cold, without the pain. I have faith in you, Johanna. I know you have the strength to do it. I know you can face the truth that Roman is gone. Will you promise me you will try?"

Knowing that Gregor loves me and has faith in me meant everything. It gave me unknown strength. Drying my eyes and straightening my body, one deep breath and my arms were around my husband promising I would try.

Things got a little better then, Stencil was able to eat more of the food we offered and the constant crying lessened. We all worked together and were proud of ourselves when we could see that the baby was stronger and putting back the weight he had lost.

As the end of February approached we began to get more sunshine and small signs of melting snow. Even so, when March arrived there was still no sign of Roman's body.

March 1, 1888, Tuesday:
For the first time there is some activity in the frozen world where we have been living for months. We had learned how to deal with the snow and ice, now we have slush. I noticed on Sunday most people were having a lot of trouble getting around. Where they had been able to walk on top of a snow bank before, now it would break through and they would be up to their waist struggling to walk.

Soon after supper one evening Gregor got up from the table to answer a knock on the door. Two young men, Jake Ripp and John Slaymaker introduced themselves and handed Gregor a small ragged coat. "We were walking across the prairie to a dance when we found this coat. We thought it might be Roman's." We all gathered around them.

"Yes, it's Roman's coat alright, boys," Gregor said. "This is the first real clue to Roman's existence anyone has found. Did you mark where you found the coat?"

"Yes," Jake answered. "We pounded a sturdy pole into the ground as hard as we could."

"I tied my blue handkerchief to it," John added. "But it may not stay there long after sunup. The ice around Schneider Hill there is beginning to melt."

Gregor was already thinking ahead of them. "Don't worry, boys. We will have a search party or two out there tomorrow morning before dawn."

     Rita L. McWhorter

A quick flurry of thanks, hand shaking and hearty slaps on the backs of the boys. Then they were off to the dance at the Castle place not far from here.

Gregor and Paul lit the lantern to show their way to Frank and Magdalena's place, knowing they would help spread the news throughout the neighborhood.

Later on we learned that Lewis Radcliff had organized another search party. They found Roman's body that had been leaning against the south side of the hill a mile east of Krobot's place which is referred to as Schneider Hill.

No one had been prepared for the condition of the body after it had been hidden under ice and snow for such a long time. When Gregor and Frank discovered the terrible stench and awful sight caused by the severe decomposition of the body they knew they could not allow anyone to see it or get close to it. Working together, they took charge of Roman's burial. Frank began by immediately building the coffin and placing the body inside. They knew I had my heart set on taking Roman into my arms for a last goodbye, but that was impossible. They decided the best solution was to nail the coffin firmly closed and bury it as soon as possible. It was kept covered under a heavy tarp in the wagon outside until the funeral.

St. Joseph Church was most considerate and the funeral was announced for immediate family only. A grave was prepared in the cemetery where the small coffin waited. A brief service was held in the church before the family gathered in the cemetery. The priest led appropriate prayers, administered the final blessings, and the coffin was lowered into the grave. It was quickly covered with sand scooped from a nearby pile.

Our now silent group went slowly back to the churchyard for a short time to exchange words of sorrow and embraces of condolence. The priest blessed us all and assured us that after so many days and weeks of grieving it was understandable that everyone must feel empty and sad.

"Now it is best to go to our separate homes to rest. Our lives will never be the same without Roman but at least we know we have done our best to see he is now safely in the hands of God in Heaven."

As tired as we were, Gregor and I talked softly together for a long time that night. We prayed that the worst was over and that we would soon have a peaceful and loving family again.

      Rita L. McWhorter

AFTERWORD

Johanna and Gregor's story continued with the promise of spring and soon Johanna was expecting another baby. On January 26, 1889 their son John Paul was born. Later they had two daughters, Mary in 1891 and Anna in 1892.

Gregor died of cancer in June of 1907 at age 55. Paul homesteaded in Wyoming where he raised a large family, and the girls all married and moved away. Stencil became a successful blacksmith, built a house in Stuart, married and fathered seven children.

John married and lived with his wife Theresa and their ten children in Johanna's dream house that had been built near the turn of the Century, a large wood frame house. The house had three 20 foot square rooms downstairs and six bedrooms upstairs. Two of the downstairs rooms had hardwood floors for dancing, the third had linoleum for the kitchen. If the house could talk it would speak to us about the weddings, parties and dances that were enjoyed at the Hytrek house. Johanna lived in the house until her last few years when she died at age 67 in April 1921.

John and Theresa had their family of ten children over a period of twenty years. Born number five in January 1926, I had three sisters and one brother; five brothers followed. We grew up during hard times when nobody had any money but we didn't know we were poor. We sang while we washed and dried the dishes, and danced when we helped care for the horses, fed the chickens and pigs, milked the cows and worked in the fields. We learned what it means to love the land and respect what nature gives us.

Today the Hytreks and their neighbors still work the farms, made possible by the dream and courage of Gregor and Johanna so long ago and the caring of those who came after them. The plow has yet to be laid down, and their work will continue, changed, but consistent, tough, tender, and true.

 Rita L. McWhorter

*Hytrek Family: Stella, Johanna holding Mary, Paul, Gregor hold-
ing John, and Stencil. About 1891. Anna was born in 1892.*

1897. Gregor and Johanna Hoffman Hytrek.

1897. Gregor and Johanna Hytrek Family. Back: Stencil, Paul, Stella, John. Front: Mary, Johanna, Anna, Gregor.

May 9, 1911. Double Wedding Reception at Gregor Hytrek's. V.J. and Anna Hytrek Krysl/Stencil and Mary Miksch Hytrek.

RITA MCWHORTER
AUTHOR BIO:

RITA L. HYTREK MCWHORTER LIVES IN DELAWARE WHERE she moved with her first husband in 1949. At age 93 she spends her time feeding birds and enjoying her children, their children, and her eleven great-grandchildren. She has traveled the world, and while this is her first published book, she has always been a writer and has inspired many others through her teaching, sharing, and skills. From her first job in a one-room schoolhouse, she has led a rich life and is gratified to be completing this story of the events and people who built her family's legacy.